MW00907534

The Bar Wench From Hell
By Gretchen Hocking

G. R. Hocking Publishing LLC
Livonia, Michigan
Barwench.hocking1@gmail.com

Editor: There are some typos in this book, I do apologize for that, and therefore will not embarrass the editor by printing her name.

Most of the names in this book have been changed in the interest of privacy.

Copyright 2010 by Gretchen Hocking, all rights reserved
Book: The Bar Wench From Hell
Date Published: 12/ 2010
GRHPCLLC:2010120001
ISBN: 978-0-9831916-0-5
Library of Congress Catalog-in-Publication Data

This book was published in the United States of America

Table of Contents

THE BAR WENCH FROM HELL

By Gretchen Hocking

HELL 101

They say I'm the Lorena Bobbitt of bartending because I'm not afraid to cut anybody off. HEY! There are worse things one could get called! How about "Shit for Brains?" That's not very flattering! Of course, you wouldn't say that to me, unless you wanted a really crumby drink. But I really prefer Bar Wench From Hell, because Bar Wench is so much less harsh. No, I'm not offended, I've earned it. Oh, don't roll your eyes back in your head, if you were in my position, you'd feel the same way. I've put up with your sorry butts and all the sorry butts that filled these seats before you were set loose from God knows where and found your way through that door, for a lot of years. What's that? You think I have an attitude? Tell ya what. Before you leave here, you won't think I have an attitude, YOU'LL KNOW I DO!!!!

OH, by the way, before I forget, don't take me too seriously, I don't. There's a lot of bar patrons I don't share that info with, so keep it to yourself. Thanks.

I'm no kid. With age, you can get away with a lot more attitude than some twenty-something punk who has yet to realize that her tits are gonna sag some day. A LOT. A lot of attitude that is, not saggy tits. People have respect for a thirty-something--

Excuse me. "Hey Bruce, sit down and shut up! It's not your day to have the remote!"

--working single mom who also happens to be in kick ass shape. I can crack open a walnut with my ass, and I don't even have to sit down. (I have yet to find anyone to believe that, but it's a good line, and I like to use it.) Alright, I'll cut the crap now, before I gag myself. They have respect for me because they have to. I have the alcohol and they don't. They all have to go through me to get a drink. My motto has always been, "Why you want to piss off the person who has the booze is beyond me." Now that you understand the ground rules, which are subject to change at my whim, I can now get back to bragging. I've earned that, too. You should also consider this a public service message, just my way of letting you know ahead of time, that if I have to hurt you, I just might be able to. Ponder that for five or ten years.

I really am in kick ass shape. If you want to challenge that, say something stupid on your way out. When you get home, you can look in the mirror and check out my footprint on your ass.

I play racquetball two or three times a week. I hit the gym four or five times a week. I took karate with my son and kickboxing with a customer who was fifteen years younger than me. What I don't take is any shit from the customers. That's you. I know what you're thinking, so let me save you the energy of having to spit it out. I've heard it a hundred times if I've heard it once:

"You're here to serve US! Not push us around and call us

names!" I do serve you people, in a VERY efficient manner. I never hesitate to point out any of your flagrant flaws before anyone else notices them and laughs. You can't get that just anyplace! I let you know when you are wrong, or when your eating skills are substandard for a public forum, or if you are ridiculously dressed, AND I pour you drinks. Seldom does anyone have to ask for anything. So yes, I do serve the customer, I just do it with attitude. Contrary to the perception of many, attitude is not a bad word.

One has to remember that people, for the most part, like order, consistency, and balance in their world. They all know I'm not Susie Sweet, but I do my job in very orderly manner. I am consistent in my attitude, and, just to balance things out, I have control of the liquor, and you don't.

"But that's not fa--"

Oh, save it. Everyone knows how they will be treated when they walk in the door. However, there are a few I like to mess with. Well, actually, everything. OH, here comes Cheryl and Jim. Just to keep Jim on his toes, I only mess with him every second or third visit. Just when he looks like he's getting comfortable, I like to pounce. "Oh, hi, Cheryl. How are ya? Hi to you, too, Shit for Brains!" (I love using that name) Before Jim can even utter a word, I ask, "That shirt looks a lot wrinkled. Did you sleep in it? Cheryl, I don't know how you put up with him!" Off they go to their table, Cheryl smiling because I said to Jim what she's been wanting to say all day, and Jim, well Jim is just looking puzzled, but that's nothing new. He just looks at Cheryl and says, "Tell me again why we come here."

Most the regulars who sit at the bar are men, so I usually band together with any of the women who are regulars. It's not any women's lib thing; it's just common sense. Any woman who is a regular at a bar, and is comfortable walking in by herself, can definitely hold her own. So even if there are only two women at the bar, and nine men, the men are still outnumbered. Any wimp guy can walk in and sit at a bar and it's socially acceptable, but if you're a woman, you'd better be tough. So guys, if you're gonna say anything stupid, be ready for major repercussions. And, in the eyes of some women, anything you say will be stupid.

Take Helen for example. (She's sort of my sidekick. Many important people throughout history have had sidekicks, Batman and Robin, Lucy and Ethel, Pinky and the Brain....) She works with mostly men at one of the auto plants. She's not afraid to walk in by herself and sit at the bar. It would be awfully lonely sitting at a table all by yourself. She doesn't do anything idiotic like try to out-drink the guys. She's too smart for that; she's got a long drive home. But she can out-smoke the best of them. She's not referred to as "Mt. St. Helen" for nothing. Oh look, here comes a new guy. This should be fun. What's that you say? How do I know it's a new guy? I know everyone in here, you fool. Now don't make me call you any more names!

"Excuse me. Is it okay if I sit here?" The new guy asks as he pulled out a bar stool two seats down from Helen, who had a drink in one hand, and a cigarette in the other, and is never phased by anything going on around her. I flew over there in a heartbeat and emphatically said "NO! Sit there!" and pointed to another seat, which happened to be right next to Mt. St. Helen.

The new guy looked at the blue haze cigarette smoke engulfing Helen and the surrounding area and said, "But I don't smoke!"

"Oh, that's okay. Helen smokes enough for two. Go ahead and sit down."

So, now the new guy, who, by the way, talks funny, gives me a look like I'm nuts. What he should have done was just walk in and sat down, instead of going through this asking shit. "I know you're new here," I continued, as I glared at him. (He's really good looking.) "But you weren't expecting special treatment, were you?" He never had time to answer. "You talk funny, where're you from?"

"A small town outside of Boston," he sheepishly replied.

"Well, I guess that explains the speech impediment. What's your name?"

"Mach."

"Mach? As in Mach One Mustang?"

He looked at me (again with the looks) like I was, well, not of this planet, "Not Mach, Maaaach."

"Could you spell that, please?" I asked him in a most polite manner.

He replied, "M A (AH) K."

"Okay," I told him. "It still sounds like 'Mach.' Why don't you try writing it down." I don't understand why he gave me such an exasperated look, but he took the pen I offered, and as he looked around for a piece a paper, I slid a bevnap in his direction.

I looked at what he wrote. M A R K. "Ohhhhhh….Maaaarrrkkk. Why didn't you say so!" I read back "M-A-R-K. You see it's an R, not an AH sound. AH, is what you say when the doctor tells you to open your mouth and stick out your tongue." (When I play doctor, I tell them to turn their head to the side and cough.)

"That's what I said!" he replied rather tersely. "M A AH K!!!"

If you're wondering why Mach isn't just throwing up his arms and walking out the door, I'll tell ya why. It's because I'm cute! Oh, what the hell! Don't choke, just live with it.

"Mach, that's Helen sitting next to you, talk to Helen. She doesn't have many friends, Helen, say hi to Mach."

"Hi, Mach! Is that Mach, like in Mustang?"

Mach just rolled his eyes back in his head, and gave a very resigned "Hello," to Helen. Mach leaned toward Helen in a conspiratorial manner and quietly asked, "Is she always like this?"

Without missing a beat, Helen replied, while blowing cigarette smoke like an old locomotive, puff, puff, puff, "Always like what?"

Mach studied Helen for a minute, and then he asked, "Are you a regular here?"

Helen continued to stare straight ahead at the television as she nodded her head and answered "Yup."

Mach then inquired, "Why do you put up with her?"

Helen stopped watching the television, turned a little sideways in her chair to face Mach, and began to explain. "Did you see her set that drink down in front of me?"

Mach looked at Helen a little quizzically and replied "Noooo..."

Helen stared at Mach and said "Neither did I. But it's always there. Did you see her empty my ashtray?"

Again Mach replied with a slow "Nooo."

"Neither did I, but it never gets full, and I smoke a lot. You see, some things in life we just don't question, and she's one of them. So, sit back, relax, and have a good time. Oh yeah, and try not to make any ignorant comments."

Mach opened his mouth to order another beer, but before he could speak, I looked at him and asked, "What's wrong with the one in front of you?"

A new beer had appeared, and he hadn't even noticed. He looked over at Helen, and again, before he could speak, she just said, "Just hold that thought."

A few minutes later, Vern sauntered in the back door. He casually said hi to Helen as walked past her to his regular seat.

"So Mach, whattya do for a living?" Helen asked, without really looking over at him as she blew her cigarette smoke straight out in front of her, in one big poof.

He cautiously replied. "I work for...(fill in your own blank, we weren't really listening). I'll be in town for a few months. What do you do?"

Helen said, "I work for GM at the parts plant. Vern over there works for Chevy. Those two guys sitting at the other end work for Ford. They're on their lunch break right now."

Mach looked at the two guys draining their beer mugs as they got up to leave. "Are they going back to work now?" he asked Helen?

"Yeah, but they've got one more break before the end of their shift, so they'll be back in a couple of hours for a quick one."

"Are they supposed to be drinking on the job?" he asked.

"They're not drinking on the job. They're drinking at the bar."

"See ya later, Helen," the two Ford guys said as they went out the door.

Helen blew the cigarette smoke out of the right side of her mouth and shouted, "Bye," towards the door. Helen is great to sit by at a picnic. You'll never get a bug bite; the surrounding smoke cloud is too thick for most insects to fly through.

Mach looked at Helen, "I was just wondering, what's the big deal about this seat anyways?"

Helen's face broke out in a big grin, as she blew her cigarette smoke out of the left side of her mouth, "Absolutely nothing. She was just seeing what you were made of." Helen sighed deeply, and then slowly released the cigarette smoke out through her nose. (I TOLD you she smoked a lot.)

The back door opened again, and in walked Sheila. "Hi, Sheila," the Bar Wench shouted, "I see you got a new dye job. God didn't give that hair color to anyone. What poodle shop did you get it from?"

Sheila just smiles and walks to her table. She knew that peach wasn't a real hair color, but she took that bold step and decided to try it anyways.

I shouted down to Mach, as I was wiping down the other end of the bar, where the two Ford guys had just vacated, "Hey Mach! You want to see a menu?"

Mach was still staring at the poodle dye job when he jerked his head in the Bar Wench's direction, then looked at Helen, "How did she know I was thinking about having some dinner, and why was she so rude to that woman with the unusual hair?"

Helen just shrugged as she exhaled smoke, yet again. When Mach turned around, there was a menu already sitting in front of him and a glaring Bar Wench. "I was not rude to Sheila. I was just making an observation."

As Mach studied the menu, he asked Helen, "What's good here?"

Helen flicked the ashes of her cigarette into the ashtray and blew more smoke out of the left side of her mouth as she answered out of the right side. "Ask her," she told Mach. Mach looked like child afraid to approach the neighborhood bully, but Helen encouraged him, "Go on. Ask her. I've never known her to bite anyone. Yet, she may throw something, but she won't bite.

And if she does, you'll be one of the chosen few. You know, like Damien." Mach sat very still as he stared into space for those two seconds of "I really hope she's just kidding.

"Oh for God's sake, Mach," he said, chastising himself for even thinking such a stupid thought. He shook it off. "OH! Wait a minute, I don't know her name, what should I call her?"

Helen snickered. "I don't know what's she's going by this week. Why don't you ask her?"

Again Mach had that "please don't make me talk to the bully" look on his face.

Helen told him, "If you don't stop showing fear, you're gonna get your jugular ripped out. Literally."

Again, Mach had that moment of "Of course she's kidding...."

"C'mon, Mach. Suck it up. You don't look like a wimp." (Actually, he looked quite good, in that dark wavy-haired Italian sort of way. Helen made a mental note to chat with the rest of the group, so they can start the pool on how long it will be before the Bar Wench starts dating this one.) "Stop acting like one."

Just as Mach was about to call me over, I stopped in front of him. "What?" I said, more a comment than a question.

He took a deep breath and stammered out, "I'm sorry. I don't know your name. What should I call you?"

I thought this over for a moment and replied, "My name is Gretchen, and that's what you may call me. Or...you may call me 'Your Highness,' I'm trying that one out this week, but so far it doesn't seem to be catching on too well, except with one of the waitresses, who wants quick service when she has a drink order."

Mach was stunned, when I actually said that in a friendly manner. "Well then, Gretchen," Mach said as he finally started to relax a little, "what would you recommend that I have for dinner this evening?"

"Since I've got a minute, let me give you my take on the menu, and don't interrupt me with stupid questions. Write down any questions you may have, and I'll answer them when I'm through with the dissertation, provided they're not too stupid to be believed."

THE MENU

"Okay, here we go, just let me take a deep breath...okay, everyone, slowly swish your beer in your mouth so you can cleanse your palette...slowly exhale...stretch...now bend to one side.... Oh, wait, I'm getting off the track here. I was slipping into yoga. Oh wait, I don't do yoga. Alright, alright, back to the menu...OH! You're going to have to listen fast. I have a lot to say in a short amount of time.

I have sampled almost every single item on the menu, including the specials, with the exception of things too disgusting to put in my mouth, like liver. It's a ritual for me to taste each of the soups every evening within ten minutes of starting my shift. If I start late, and the regulars point it out to me, then I have to tell them to go thirsty while I run over to get a soup sample.

This sampling is not just gluttony on my part. It also falls under Research and Development. Being able to critique any menu item is a service most have come to appreciate. If you are wondering what my critique for the liver would be, it is "People all over the world have eaten liver, and lived to talk about it. Those who have had the liver here tell me it is fine. If you order it with bacon, I will have a piece of bacon."

"I don't like liver," Mach somehow managed to squeeze in.

"What did I tell you about interruptions?" WHACK!!! Out of nowhere a menu hit Mach upside the head. "Have you slowed down or are you still listening quickly?"

IS THE FISH FRESH, SOME FOOL WHIIIIIINED…

"Michigan IS 'The Great Lake State.' Your chances of getting fresh fish here are pretty good. I'd say your chances are better here than in the middle of Arizona. If you have to ask me why, I may have to whack you again." Mach gave a little involuntary shudder.

"However, if you want a lobster tail, and are a complete geographical idiot, then that is fresh, too. Here's another clue. If you are walking in the back door of the restaurant, and you see the fish delivery truck in the parking lot, then fish would be a good choice for the evening, unless you are allergic to it, in which case I would make a different selection.

"(Now we're off into ramble land, me that is. You can hang in there, or close your eyes while you are reading. It makes no difference to me.) A snappy answer I have always enjoyed using when one inquires about the freshness of the fish is: "Yes, we just caught it at Newburgh Lake this afternoon." Newburgh Lake is a small man-made lake about a quarter of a mile down the road. It was drained at one point in time to clean all the sludge, grunge, beer cans and chemical refuse from the bottom. If lakes were likened to body parts, this one would be an arm pit. Of an unbathed specimen. If you believed, even for a fraction of a second, that we served fish caught in Newburgh Lake, then let me recommend the Grilled Carp with Mercury Sauce.

"Hey!!! I see you making faces over there Beverly; don't get mad at me because you fell for the Grilled Carp crap."

Mach held his hand up as if to try and interject something, all he got out was "What abo.."

"Helen, handle this." Without ever taking her eyes off of the television, she backhanded him in the arm. Now I can continue.

APPETIZERS

"Let me start by saying that there are a few appetizers that show up on many menus that I find anything but appetizing.

"The first is escargot. For those who have never been in a restaurant kitchen to see the actual preparation of these gnarly little wads of bottom feeders, let me tell you, there isn't anyone back there gently prying the aforementioned wads out of their cute little snail shells. THEY COME IN CANS!!! Then they are unceremoniously dropped into their cute little nooks, in their cute little metal dish, (for lack of a better word), and said metal dish is tossed onto a burner with enough butter to clog the arteries of four sumo wrestlers and enough garlic to mask the odor of the skunk that sprayed your dog while you were standing next to it. Thennn...when the cook has determined that the little metal dish is hot enough to cause first degree burns if touched by bare skin, (or if a wooden skewer burns), he grabs his tongs and plops the container on a plate, wipes up any spilled garlic butter in a half-ass manner, and sends it on its way. Your server will then grab some bread on the fly, hope to hit the plate on the first try, and majestically serve you your escargot while the butter is sizzling hot. Gee, I hope it doesn't splatter you. Every time someone orders these chewy snot wad balls you hear the same crap:

Mmmmmmmmm....I love escargot.......I especially like the garlic butter.....Oh! These are wonderful......You guys have the best escargot here.......Here, have one.......Oh, you've gotta try one...."

Everyone who orders this stuff is always trying to get you to have one! "I DON'T WANT ONE!!!" I tell them LOUDLY and CLEARLY!

"But you've got to try it!" They always whine back at me.

"No, I don't have to try it!" I tell them, again with the LOUD and CLEAR outdoor voice.

"But you're supposed to try everything at least once" This line is always said in an authoritative whine, if there is such a thing.

"Well then, if we follow your logic," I ask the snot wad chewing idiots, "will you try some deep fried dog balls if we bring them in tomorrow?"

"Oh Yuck ! That's disgusting!" As if looking at snails aren't.

"But they're soooooo goooood." I guess we're back to whining about he escargot. I never understood this type of logic. If they are SO GOOD, then why don't you just eat them all yourself? There's only six! AND....if it's the garlic butter you like so much, then save the money on the escargot and ask for garlic butter and bread!

OYSTERS

Oh yuck!! These are even more unappealing than the escargot. Yes, they are actually served on the shell--Oh, excuse me. 'Half shell'--after one of the kitchen help pries them open with a screwdriver and a hammer. I'm not kidding! Then they are placed on a bed of ice. How nice. I bet the oysters are real thrilled about that too. Let us not forget the lemon! Why don't you try to squirt the lemon in its eye, so it goes blind?

Everyone says that you don't chew them; you just let them slide down your throat. I think that seems like a good way to choke. You can't chew them; they're too chewy. I don't eat meat that's too chewy, so why would I want to take a chance on choking on some dead blob of ocean matter that some say is similar to a wad of snot sliding down your throat. Just breathe on me and give me a cold instead. I'll supply my own snot."

"What do they taste like?"

"There's really not much flavor."

"So what's the point in eating them?"

"They're an aphrodisiac."

"Not to those watching you eat them."

CAJUN SHRIMP

"Try the cajun shrimp. It's great.

"While we are on the subject of appetizers, just why are these things called appetizers in the first place?!? Put your hand down, Mach. It was a rhetorical question. I've always found that once I start eating, my appetite doesn't increase, it does just the opposite and decreases. Isn't that the object of eating? To DECREASE the hunger pangs? I've never eaten a plate of Cajun shrimp and said, "Wow, I'm hungrier than ever! Excuse me! Waitress...May I double my dinner order, please? Those appetizers sure did what they were named for!"

"The dictionary says an appetizer is something served before the main course of a meal to stimulate the appetite. The only thing that can be stimulated by the "Bovine Sampler Platter" of deep fried delicacies such as chicken parts (wings or fingers, which they keep in their little vest pockets), mushrooms, cheese sticks, and potato skins is the clogging of the last artery you still had use of.

"Don't let me put a damper on your Friday evening 'Food-a-rama.' I hope the appetizers enhanced your appetite enough so you have room for the 'Heart Smart' extra large portion of Prime Rib, and don't trim the fat off."

SHRIMP COCKTAIL

"I wasn't exactly sure whether 'shrimp cocktail' technically fell under the appetizer category but, that tired old dictionary says:

An appetizer typically consisting of seafood or mixed nuts. Go figure. A quick F.Y.I. for those who may have had a few of the OTHER kind of cocktails, do not try to drink a 'shrimp cocktail,' unless you have already run it through your Jack Lalane juicer. Don't roll your eyes back at me! There ARE people stupid enough to try and drink this! Right now, I think they're eating escargot.

"Okay, enough about appetizers for right now, let's get to the main menu.

"Mach, are you keeping up with me? What about the rest of you?"

ITALIAN FOOD

"We have a few Italian dishes on the menu, such as spaghetti, lasagna, baked mostoccioli, and occasionally a few different variations of fettuccine. So, of course, people are going to ask if the sauce is any good. After all, this is a beef place. So I tell them that the sauce is wonderful. The owner is Italian, he's actually from Italy, and he brought his 93 year old grandmother over here to show him how to make the sauce and to put together the best lasagna in the world. Once he mastered the sauce, he was going to send Grandma home, but she didn't want to go; she wanted to stay and help. For a while, she was actually crushing the grapes for the house wine with her bare feet, until the "Slip and Fall." Now she just runs over the grapes with the wheels of her walker."

MEXICAN FOOD

"I can remember when there was only one Mexican restaurant in this area, and I had never been there. But slowly, Mexican food got to be very popular, so the Boss went with the flow and added nachos, burritos, tostadas, and of course chips and cheese with salsa to the menu. You can tell the salsa is homemade. It never has the same 'heat value' two weeks in a row. I used to get a monkey dish of salsa and either tortilla chips or crackers when I had a cold. If the salsa was in 'fires of Hell' mode, you didn't have to bother with any over-the-counter decongestants."

OH PLEASE, NAME THE NACHOS AFTER ME....

"Hang in there; we're still talking about Mexican food.

"We who are here to serve the public will often go the extra yard to make them happy. Yeah, right. So 'Hold the pickles, hold the lettuce, special orders don't upset us....' No, we don't have Whoppers you idiot. This isn't Burger King... One little song and some people lose it. Gee, let's give them more alcohol.

"Mach, you've got to stop interrupting me by raising your hand. If you have any questions, write them down. If you have to use the restroom, it's the last door on the left, but you may not get up until I am finished, which will happen a lot sooner if you just keep quiet and listen."

"But I'm not interested in Mexican food," he somehow managed to squeeze in.

"I don't recall asking if you were. Anyways, Noreen always ordered her nachos without the meat. After about a year of ordering this way, and she had them EVERYTIME she came, she got this bright idea, and asked if the Veggie Nachos could be named after her. She thought Noreen's Nachos had a nice ring.

"She thought wrong."

This time in his interruption, Mach directed it towards Helen, "She's veering off the subject here," he said behind his hand. Like that was real sneaky. Again Mach got backhanded, but this time it was accompanied by a small cloud of smoke.

"One Friday evening, as Noreen was sitting there with the rest of the Friday Night Supper Club, she decided to start a petition to have the nachos without meat named after her. She reached over and borrowed some of our best bar stationary (bevnaps) to state her cause, and then had all those around her sign it. She asked if I would sign it. Fool.

"I said, 'Sure, I'd love to sign your petition.' She was thrilled. I took her petition and scribbled my John Hancock on there. I even did so with a flourish, dramatically waving my hand in the air after I dotted my 'i.' (NO, there's no 'i' in Gretchen, I'm talking about my last name, stupid!) Noreen was gleaming!!!

"'Hey look everyone, she signed my petition!!!'

"You know, it feels good to do something so simple that can make someone else so happy. The rest of the group was really surprised that I signed it. They were bobbing their heads in amazement. Except for Dave, he knew there had to be a catch.

"With the joy still on her face, and the rest of the crowd congratulating her on a job well done, I set the petition down in the ash tray and lit it. Boy, those bevnaps sure burn fast."

THE PICTURE MENU

"The picture menu is used mainly for our late night customers, who asked too many bothersome questions because they were too lazy to read the Night Owl Menu. I was always prepared to help them with the big words or any word they may have deemed foreign, like spaghetti. But too often, they would sit and whine about not knowing what they wanted or were too tired to think, yada, yada, yada. So, I came up with a solution to make things easier for them, The Picture Menu.

"I etched a crude version of this menu on the back of a place mat, then took my ideas home and had my then nine year old son draw the final draft. He was a far better artist than I. Representing the beef selections that were offered was of course a lovely drawing of a cow. For the pasta or Italian selections that were available was an appetizing drawing of a plate of spaghetti. The Mexican dishes were denoted by a Mexican wearing a poncho and a sombrero, and should you decide upon a fish or seafood entrée, you simply pointed to the illustration of a fish.

"The Picture Menu was meant to simplify things, so any questions I feel are unnecessary will not be tolerated. One patron decided on the fish one night, and hence, pointed to the fish illustration. That was sufficient. But then he had the arrogance to ask 'What kind of fish is it?' I had to nip this in the bud. I had to point out a few things to him, like, it was LATE, you're all power drinking because you have a limited amount of time before I throw your sorry butts out of here, and you just pointed at picture of a fish!!! How picky can you get! Be happy you're getting food!!

"He said the fish would be fine, went back to drinking his beer and watching M*A*S*H reruns."

DON'T TOUCH THAT PLATE! IT'S HOT!

"A variety of foods are served on metal platters or plates that have come right out of the oven. It keeps the food hot and saves the cook the nightmare of having to transfer certain dishes to another plate. Some foods are just not very cooperative when trying to slide them onto another plate. They definitely would not look as appetizing, like Baked Mostoccioli for instance. If you tried to slide it on to another plate that DIDN'T just come out of the oven, the cheese would most certainly get stuck at some point during the sliding process, and then the pasta would tumble out, and then the cook would try and put the cheese back on top, but it would have dents in it and look like a "re-serve" (you know, like when you re-gift something) or you would be certain that it went to the wrong table first, someone stuck their fork it, dug around, and realized it wasn't theirs, and then so on and so forth, and we'd have to listen to your obnoxious whining, and then I'd have to hit you upside the head, so we serve it on the hot platter, which sits on a hot platter holder. (I don't know the technical term.) Then we tell you, 'THE PLATTER IS HOT!!!'And what do you do ???? YOU TOUCH THE PLATTER!!!!

"OUCH !!! That platter is really hot!"

"I TOLD you it was, and not to touch it, you moron!"

"Yeah, but I didn't think it was that hot."

"Why would we bother telling you it was hot if it wasn't hot?"

"Well, I thought it might be a little warm, you know, to keep the food warm."

"I didn't say the platter is warm, you moron, I said it was HOT!"

"Yeah, but...."

"AND I told you not to touch it. So what's the first thing you do? You touch it!! When you were a kid, you got your tongue stuck to the flagpole in winter, and stuck a fork in an electrical outlet, didn't you?"

Just as abruptly as I started, I finished, and walked away with the drinks I was making while explaining the menu to Mach. Mach turned towards Helen, and before he could even get the words out, she just stared back and said, "You asked." She loudly exhaled a large cloud of smoke. Mach was starting to see shapes forming in Helen's cigarette smoke clouds, like fluffy little bunnies. (I hope he keeps this to himself.) He got a little defiant with Helen and said, "You set me up!!"

She broke out into a huge grin and agreed with him, "Yeah, I sure did."

"What are you her sidekick?" Mach was asking this just as Vern got bored and decided to move down by Helen and him. He sat on the other side of Helen, as he did that Helen leaned back in her chair and introduced Vern and Mach.

"Hi, Vern, nice to meet you."

"Hi Mach, is that Mach like in Mustang?"

"Why is everyone asking... Yes, yes it is. I was conceived in the back seat of a Mustang."

Helen gave Mach an admiring look, and patted him on the shoulder. "You know, Mach, you're not as dumb as you look."

"Thank you, Helen. I appreciate that. Hey, wait a minute.... Oh no, you're just like her" He pointed to me just when he was finally starting to relax. Helen just grinned and blew smoke rings.

"Mach, let me tell you. Helen is no one's sidekick," Vern emphatically informed him. "She's an entity all to herself. But if these two should ever team up, heaven help us all!"

"Hey, Vern, got any suggestions about what I should have for dinner?"

Vern quickly replied, "I'll tell you what NOT to have! Don't order anything to go!"

"I wasn't going to, but why not?"

Just as suddenly as I disappeared, I was back in front of Mach, "I'll tell you why."

THE CARRY OUT

"When Vern was working the midnight shift, he would

occasionally come in on his break, somewhere around 1:00 a.m. One night he decided to take a burger back to work, so he could have it for lunch, whatever time that was at.

"When it gets to be late, and there are just a few patrons, I sometimes do the cooking myself, as long as it's easy. I can handle a well done burger with grilled onions. Boy, that really sounds good right now, I thought. I couldn't eat an entire half pound burger right then. It's too late. Maybe, I'll just take a bite out of Vern's.

"So there I was, cooking this fabulous burger, being enticed by the aroma of the grilled onions, giving my olfactory senses a real treat. A bite would taste reeeeaallllly good right now. That's all I want, just one bite. That will cure my burger craving. Besides that, he deserves it, for reasons too numerous to mention. I haven't had a burger with grilled onions in a long time. Oooohhhhh…it's going to be hot! Right off the grill, freshly grilled bun, onions cascading over the sides…okay, it's ready… time to put it on the bun…smell smell smelllll…yuummmmm. Time to put it in the to-go box, but FIRST!!! A detour to my mouth!

"The burger suddenly swooped upward, as if it had wings, and firmly implanted itself in my mouth! (That's my story and I'm stickin' to it)

"WOW!! Is that ever hot! Does this ever taste great! WHOA! Still hot! Oh, delicious! Shit! Still hot! Quick, finish chewing before I go back behind the bar. Damn! Still hot! Okay, pack up the burger, put it in the bag, almost done chewing, savoring the flavor…Okay, got the ketchup and mustard packets in the bag, got the napkin, all done swallowing, close up the bag….and back behind the bar.

"Mission accomplished. I put the bag next to Vern; he finished his beer and headed back to work.

"Same scene at the bar, different night. Vern comes in on his break for a couple of quick ones. He relaxes for a minute, and then starts the conversation with—I point at Vern, okay Vern, you take it from here."

Vern nodded and picked up the story without missing a beat. "The other night at work, I told this guy I had a half pound burger, but wasn't hungry enough to eat the whole thing, so I asked him if he wanted half of it. He said sure, he'd take half a burger. So, I open up the bag, pull out the to-go box, open it up to reveal a burger with a big ol' bite missing out of it!"

He said his buddy looked at him like he was nuts, why would he even consider eating a carry out burger that someone had already started on! He had to explain that it was a good friend of his that did this, and it was in retaliation for something he had done, and yes, he did deserve it.

"But it's got a bite out of it! It's a used burger!" Obviously this guy needs to get a life. I didn't spit on it, I just took a bite. And I don't even wear lipstick, so there's no waxy residue. The look on Vern's face when he told us about discovering the missing bite was truly a Kodak moment, but it probably wasn't as much fun as watching the horrified expression on his buddy's face when he started eating the "used burger."

I savored that moment even more than I savored the delicious bite of that burger. When all was said and done, the explanation didn't matter, the guy did not want part of a used burger.

RACQUETBALL

Mach was still looking at the menu when Jason came in. Jason usually had dinner with us four or five nights a week. (I TOLD you the food was good!) And if you're wondering why this chapter is called "Racquetball," you'll soon find out. You really need to show a little patience. And no, I'm not that far off track. Mach has not yet made a decision as to what he'll have for dinner, but I can't just stand here and wait for him to decide. "Hey Mach, if you're having trouble with the big words, just ask Helen. She'll tell you what they are, or just make them up. But either way, you won't know the difference."

Jason sat in his usual seat, at the end of the bar nearest the kitchen. Given the "L" shape of the bar, this put him perpendicular to Helen, Mach, and Vern.

"Hi, Jase," Helen said as she waved to him.

Vern added, "What's up Jase?"

I went over and abruptly hit him upside the head with the menu. "You owe me a dollar!"

Vern and Helen started laughing, and Mach just looked back forth between from Helen and Vern to Jason, like he was watching a tennis match. Mach decided to hold his head still for a moment and asked Helen, "Why did she hit him with..." But before he could finish Helen cut in, "Shhhh," as she gave him a warning glare, "Or you'll be..." WHACK! Too late, Mach got hit upside the head with the menu.

He was stunned. "What did you do that for?"

I just casually shrugged. "I wasn't aware I needed a reason. Alright, back to that dollar we were discussing before the foreign guy interrupted me."

"I'm not a foreigner," Mach protested, "I'm from..." WHACK!!!!

Mach decided to hold that thought.

You see, Jason and I got in to the habit of playing racquetball twice a week. He worked across the street and down a little, and the racquetball courts were across the street and down a little in the opposite direction. How convenient. So, we would meet at 10:00 in the morning and slap the ball around the court.

Jason, being a very cooperative soul, and a MUCH better racquetball player than I, found a way to even out the game and make it more interesting. We bet. But then, here at the bar, we bet on everything. We developed a "stair step" scale of how I could win money. First of all, we would play until the first player hit 21. It was always Jason; however, if I scored five points, I would win a dollar. If I was lucky enough to score ten points, I would win two dollars, and three for fifteen. If I actually won a game, I would win five dollars. The only way that could actually happen would be if Jason was on crutches, lost his racquet, was wearing a blindfold and playing on another court. Even then, I may not have gotten to 21 points. I do believe one of the challenges that Jason set for himself was to ease up a bit until I got to four points, and then spend the rest of the game not letting me get to five. Through some fluke, I usually ended up with a dollar. Yes, I am going somewhere with this. I'm going right back to the bar, where payment of said dollar usually takes place. As the rest of the patrons watched, Jason, in a very disgruntled manner, would pull out a dollar and slowly hand it to me. Jason was a WONDERFUL sport and never rained on my parade. As I skipped over to put the dollar in my tip jar, the guys at the bar would all stare at Jason. He would just shrug and say, "What can I tell you? She's tough."

Mach was once again a little confused. He asked Vern and Helen, "Is she really that good?"

Mach quickly jerked his head straight forward as he heard me ask him, "Have you ever played racquetball before?"

"I've played a couple of times, about ten years ago."

"I'll kick your ass," I said in passing, and this was said with the utmost of confidence.

Mach looked down at Jason, as Jason asked him, "You've

only played a couple of times?"

"Yeah, it was a while ago."

"She'll kick your ass. I can also tell you what she's going to wear because you'll be distracted every time she bends over to serve the ball."

Jason was sooooo good for my image. This really had Mach wondering. The rest of the bar was smirking. They've been through this before. You see, I really would kick Mach's ass, but only because I choose my opponents wisely. I can beat anyone who has never really played racquetball, and two times ten years ago isn't gonna help him out now. As Mach was still pondering his next comment, Jason gave him same sage advice. "If you play, don't bet big."

"But I wasn't going to bet."

Jason got a half grin on his face. "You will if you play."

One evening when a few of us were talking about racquetball, one guy thought he would be clever and butt in. He told me, "Don't let your mouth write a check your ass can't cash." That was Skip shooting his mouth off. While he was still feeling smug, I told him, "Hold on a second while I bend over, and you can kiss mine."

Let us share with everyone the story of Skip. Skip thought, because he played tennis, that he could play racquetball equally as well. Skip thought wrong. I told him I would kick his ass. Jason told him I would kick his ass. The ENTIRE bar told him I would kick his ass. I kicked his ass. The conversation at the bar after said match went something like this:

"How many games did you play?" (The crowd anxiously wanted to know)

"We played four games," I told them, ever so casual and calm.

"How much money did you make?" (Inquiring minds want to know)

"I made twenty dollars."

"Then that means that Skip lost a total of one hundred dollars. He made the same bet with four of us that he was gonna win."

"I got my money. I hope you guys don't have to hold him upside done to empty his pockets out." He just had to shoot his mouth off and learn the hard way. We tried to tell him that racquetball was different from tennis.

"Hmmm. Expensive lesson."

"Yeah, too bad."

"Okay, everyone in unison now.......ASS HOLE!"

"Oh look everyone! Here comes 'Skippy' now!"

"Hey Skippy, did you stop at the bank before you came here? You do know we only take cash."

"Hey Bar Wench!! How many points did you let Skippy have?"

"He had as many in three games as I had in one."

Skippy jumped in. "Yeah well, what about the third game?!? I had seven points in the third game!! He sounded very defensive as he was waving around five fingers on one and two on the other.

"Skippy, I gave you two of those points."

"YOU DID NOT!! HOW?!?!?!?"

"Remember when the ball came off the front wall and hit me?"

"Yeah, man, I really smoked that one!"

"You didn't smoke anything. I had time to casually step in front of the ball. I was getting bored." I wouldn't be bragging too hard. "That's still less than half. It's not like any of the games were close. I barely broke a sweat. We could have mopped up the court with you. Oh, wait a minute! I did!!! HAHAHAHAHAHAHAHAHAHAHAHA." (Hey! I never said I was subtle)Skippy just walked back to his table as the rest of the bar guffawed, and each winner bought a round with their winnings.

Mach pulled an ostrich and stuck his face back in the menu. He finally decided to try and order some dinner. He looked up as I was pouring a beer. "Excuse me, Gretchen. May I order something?"

"Sure, order anything you want."

"Well, I had a question about the specials."

"Mach, everything here is special."

"I'll just have a grilled chicken sandwich and some fries." Then he looked over at Helen and Vern. "There. That wasn't so bad."

"Hey Mach!" the Bar Wench yelled from the other end. "Do

you want that regular or Cajun?"

"What's regular?"

"Not Cajun," I shouted.

Vern just rolled his eyes back in his head. "You had to know that was coming."

Mach gave a series of resigned nods. "I guess I'll have that Cajun."

"Mach," said the Bar Wench as she let out a sigh, "This is no time to be wishy-washy, do you guess or do you know if you want it Cajun? I'm not a mind reader, you know."

"YES! I'll have it Cajun!"

"Oh, good for you, do want it mild Cajun or hot Cajun?" At this, Helen and Vern both let a small chuckle explode out of their mouths before they caught themselves.

Mach decided to be clever. "I'll have it however you like it. I'll trust your recommendation."

I smiled directly at Mach and told him, "What a great idea. I hate taking a bite out of things I don't like." And with that she whirled around and headed off to get a place setting.

Vern and Helen were still doing one of those silent laughs, you know, where you sort of snort out of your nose. Mach stared at them, not because they were laughing, but because he had to know if the Bar Wench was serious about taking a bite out of his food. "I thought you said she only did that with carry outs?!?"

Vern stopped laughing for a moment, but he sure had a wide grin. "I didn't say it was only carry outs. I just mentioned there was a bite missing in mine. Oh!!! I know what you're worried about. Don't worry. She'll let you take the first bite! But only on your first time eating here."

When Mach looked down towards where Jason was sitting, he saw the Bar Wench take a french fry off Jason's plate. Again, he turned his attention to Vern and Helen, "Does she eat everyone's food?!?"

Helen blandly replied, "If you don't want her to test your food, you have to order something she doesn't like."

"Well, what doesn't she like?"

"Liver!," they both answered in unison.

"Is that it? Because I don't like liver, either."

"Oh well, happy dining!"

Things went relatively smooth for Mach throughout the dining process. Although he was apprehensive each time I passed by him, he'd flinch a little and put his hands up as if to guard his food. I didn't touch it. That would be too predictable. I'll wait until his guard is down.

Now that Mach was done eating, he went on a limb and asked the Bar Wench, "Why do you sample everyone's food?"

"Quality control, it's in the job description," she said over her shoulder from the service bar as she was pouring a Manhattan.

"So, Mach," Helen said, "are you gonna be here tomorrow night?"

"Probably. I'll be staying at the hotel right behind here, and since it's only a short walk across the parking lot, I won't have to worry about drinking and driving. Besides that, I don't know of anyplace else to go yet. What's this place like on Friday? Does it get very busy?"

"Yeah, it's packed on Fridays." Helen explained, "If you want to get a seat at the bar, you better do some quick sucking up so the Bar Wench will find you a seat tomorrow."

"Why is it up to her whether I get a seat or not?"

"How do birds fly, and why do we have rainbows? Mach, Mach, Mach, you've really got to stop being so naïve. Friday night becomes standing room only. Trust me. This place will be a zoo tomorrow night. If you want any chance of getting a seat, you'll have to depend on her to tell who's leaving next, where you should stand, or who to vulture over so they will leave. And then when someone starts to leave, you better have half a cheek sliding onto that bar stool before the person vacating it is all the way off."

"Wow. That sounds like a lot of work just to sit down."

"It's not," Helen told him. "Not if you lay the proper ground work ahead of time."

"Okay, so what do I do to get on her good side?"

"Tell her hair looks good."

"You've got to be kidding me!"

Just then, Kelly, the hostess, was walking by with an arm full of menus. Helen turned around in her seat to stop Kelly, "Hey Kelly, let me borrow one of those menus for a second."

Kelly stopped and said "Oh sure," and handed Helen a menu. Whack! Helen promptly hit Mach upside the head with the menu and handed it back to Kelly. "Thanks Kelly."

"No problem." With that done, Kelly wandered back to the hostess station.

Mach just sat there staring at Helen with his mouth hanging wide open. "What was that for?!? Am I in the Twilight Zone?!? Are you on the payroll?"

Helen calmly sat there and once again took Mach under her wing and explained, "You need to stop asking so many questions and learn to listen. I'm telling you, if you don't want to eat standing up tomorrow, you'll take out seat insurance now and tell her that her hair looks good."

Mach looked around Helen at Vern. "Have you ever been hit with a menu?"

Vern nodded his head and grinned. "About once a week for the last fifteen years. You do the math. Although I think you may be working on a new one night record. And, by the way, sad as it is, Helen is right. If you want a seat tomorrow, do as she says. Don't worry. It gets easier, they're just trying to break you in."

As the Bar Wench approached, Mach hesitatingly said, "Ah excuse me, ah, Gretchen, or--I mean, Your Highness, I just wanted to say, I think your hair looks really good tonight."

"Why thank you, Mach! Are you going to be joining us tomorrow evening?"

"Yeah, I was planning on it."

"Make sure you catch my attention when you get here, and I'll get you seated just as soon as possible." I had actually overheard the entire conversation. C'mon, this place isn't that big. Besides, Mach was toooooooo good looking to let get away this early in the game.

"Hey, Bar Wench!" shouted Vern, "Did you set your hair with fire crackers today?"

WHACK!!! Vern just got the menu upside the head. He looked over at Mach, "See what I mean? I guess my night is complete. I gotta run. See you guys later."

As Vern was leaving, Wendell, who's afraid of his own shadow and looks like the stereotypical fellow with spectacles who gets sand kicked in his face, was trying to sneak out along side of Vern. "Hey Wendell," I yelled over to him. (His sneaking wasn't too good,) "You wanna be my enchilada? I can make your salsa hot!"

Wendell gets all embarrassed and shit, next thing you know he careens off the wall because he was trying to hide his head by looking down. Works every time! The best, though, was the time he bounced off of the wall, right into Loretta's tits. I never knew anyone could turn that shade of red and without needing life support.

"You know, Mach, if you stick around a little while longer, you'll be here for Complimentary Cracker Night," Helen said in between puffs.

"What the hell is Complimentary Cracker Night?"

"The Bar Wench passes out free crackers."

"What's so great about free crackers?"

"It's not just the crackers, Mach. It's a tradition."

"I think I've absorbed enough of this place for one night. For my first night. I really need to go."

A few minutes later, as Mach was leaving, he said, "Bye Helen, nice talking to you. Are you usually here after work?"

"Yeah, but I don't get off for another two and a half hours. I work afternoons."

It took a moment for Mach to process this. "But if you work afternoons, shouldn't be at work right now?!?"

"Yeah, but I forgot to go back after my first break."

Jason noticed that for the first time in years, Helen didn't have a cigarette or two burning in the ashtray. "Hey Helen, did you cut back on smoking?"

"As a matter of fact, I did. Thanks for noticing."

"No problem. What are you down to?"

"Three packs a day."

"Good girl."

Mach just walked out shaking his head, absently rubbing it where he had been hit by the menu. I stopped to chat with Helen once things slowed down a little. Helen made the comment, "Mach is one good looking guy."

"Yes, he is," I concurred.

"So," Helen said, "are you interested? Is he going to make the cut?"

"Time will tell, Helen. Time will tell." Then I leaned over and conspiratorially told her, "Bet on a week from Sunday." I like to give Helen the heads up. She's won so many Bar Wench bets the rest of the group thinks she's psychic. NO, not psycho, you buffoon, I said PSYCHIC.

ENTER THE MORON BROS.

(I'm not going to give these guys their own chapter)

Don't get your skirt all tied up in a knot thinking it's mean that we should call two guys the Moron Bros. Believe me, if you met them you'd be thinking, "Wow, they're really taking it easy on them."

Every Thursday when they stomped through the door, they would be arguing. Usually they were arguing about ice cream. (Don't ask) As soon as they walked about half way down the bar, they would then be finished arguing, and would give each other the silent treatment. (Boy, that'll teach him.) One would've thought they were having a lovers quarrel. IF they both sat at the bar, they would leave an empty seat between them. When asked about the empty seat, one or the other would very defensively reply, "It would look funny if we sat next to each other."

"Why? No one else looks funny sitting next to anyone else."

"You know, we don't want people to think we're--"

"That you're what? Incredible homophobes? Idiots?"

It was so obvious that they were brothers, and even more

obvious that they were morons.

If they were REALLY mad at each other, then one or the other would go sit at a table, and one at the bar. I then shouted to the one at the table, "HEY whattya having tonight?"

True to form he would ignorantly reply, "Aren't you supposed to come over to the table and take my order?" Stupid, stupid question.

I tried a different approach. "Is your brother too mad to drive you to the emergency room?"

"Why would I want to go to the emergency room?"

Another stupid question.

"Because if you ask me another foolish question like the first one, I'm gonna come over there and break your face with a condiment tray. After they remove the feeding tube and super glue your teeth back in place, you'll be able to take nourishment through a straw. Now, this is your last chance, whattya gonna have?"

"Coke."

"We went through all that for a fuckin' Coke!?!?!?!?"

See, we weren't being mean calling them the Moron Brothers. Please think before you speak lest we consider you one of their cousins.

If they sit anywhere near Helen, she'll power smoke (that's like chain smoking, only faster) and keep blowing the smoke in their direction. If Phil (You've never met him) is here, he'll grab a menu and try to aid the process by fanning the smoke in the direction of the Brothers Moron.

The brother at the bar, who was oblivious to the smoke, suddenly perked up and asked, "Are we in time for Cracker Night?"

COMPLIMENTARY CRACKER NIGHT

Every Thursday, at ten o'clock sharp, is Complimentary Cracker Night. Just before ten o'clock, the patrons like to do a little count down, you know, like New Year's Eve, and then we have the tossing of the crackers. (I've told them time and time again to get a life) What's that you say? Aren't the crackers usually free? Of course, they come with the soup, but what if no one is having soup? AHA! Are we supposed to feed the entire clientele for free? There may be upward of twelve or fourteen people in here at that time!!!

Some are at the bar, and everyone at the bar is automatically included, whether they want to be or not. Some are at a table, but do not want to be left out of Complimentary Cracker Night so we include those who wish to participate. Or not. (It's a big draw) Okay, here's the routine: those who are in the know about Complimentary Cracker Night start talking about it ten or fifteen minutes before ten. Then they start bugging me to get the crackers ready. How, you're wondering, does one get the crackers ready? Don't they come in wrapped in little, hermetically sealed packages? Yes, they do, but they are not going to fly to the customers by themselves. Really, stop trying to over simplify

Cracker Night! At the stroke of ten, I stand at the center of the bar, with an armful of crackers, carefully counted out to match the exact number of patrons that are participating, and when they all yell GO!!!... I throw the crackers to them as quickly as possible. A number of things can and always do go wrong. First of all, crackers are NOT good projectiles. IF you try and throw them farther than three feet, (which I do), they start to veer off course. Sometimes they are dramatically off course and hit someone in the head. (Oh well) Sometimes they land in someone's drink, in which case I get bonus points, and everyone whose drink wasn'thit cheers.

There are times when some try to catch the flying crackers, and upon grabbing them out of the air, they break the crackers, in which case they are not eligible to turn them in for new, pristine, unbroken crackers. Perhaps they should have just waited for the crackers to hit them in the face and put their eye out. The eye thing might be a little irritating, but at least they would have unbroken crackers. Sometimes you just have to weigh your options. Helen likes to build up the haze of smoke around her, so it's more of a challenge to catch the crackers for her and those around her. She is pretty amazing though. She rarely misses as she snags the flying crackers out of mid-air as she exhales while holding her cigarette with the inch and a half ash on it in her stationary hand. Sometimes it is like watching some kid play jacks, as she snags two packs out of the air. SNAG! SNAG! It was actually quite impressive. The junior Moron Brother is still wondering what happened to his crackers last week when he had to sit next to Helen.

It really used to piss me off when she would then put her cigarette out on the freshly caught package of crackers. But I found a use for it. Inevitably some idiot would ask if was okay to eat the crackers. I would quickly bark back, "NO, you can't eat those. They're not broken. They're not even cracked," as I snatched the crackers out of his hand before he knew what was happening. Then I would magnanimously tell him, "Here, you can have eat these crackers," as I handed him the ones that Helen had put her cigarette out on. "Just eat around the part where the plastic wrapper adhered to the crackers when the cigarette burnt through it. Look, there's not even any ash on them!"

I keep trying to tell people that staring with their mouth wide open, looking like Goofy would just after he smoked a party size doobie, is not at all conducive to the rest of the crowd thinking them intelligent.

"Close your mouth, it's a tough crowd. They're gonna go for the jugular."

For all who are wondering, I'll tell you how Cracker Night got started: I was bored.

For all who are wondering what the point of this is, there isn't any point. No point at all. And if you are still scratching your head, well, I bet you do that a lot.

ANATOMY OF A FRIDAY NIGHT
(Okay, so the menu gig is over)

Friday nights are great! It's busy from the word go. There isn't even a remote possibility that it could get boring. There's no time to get bored. Punching in on a Friday is like hitting the "Showtime Clock." From the moment you punch the clock, you have the thirty second walk through the kitchen to the bar to get your game face on. You have to start the night out right, so you can't have some stupid smile on your face that says, "Oh, I'm so happy to see all you morons!" You have to come out swinging with your "Don't mess with me" smile, which some have said is more a sneer, than a smile. Yeah, and Mona Lisa is laughing.

As I turn the corner and strut behind the bar, I'm greeted with many a "Hey, Bar Wench, how's it going tonight?" My standard reply is, "Kickin' ass first and takin' names later." The meeker ones just manage a barely audible, "Hi."

Standard reply, "NO! Are you?!?" The ones who ponder that too long are usually poor "Wheel of Fortune" players also.

The crowd murmurs, "Another Friday, and all's right with the world."

You learn through experience how to stay six steps ahead of the game. When you have four waitresses shouting out drink orders to you at once, you start at the far end and gather up all the bottled beer you need for everyone, then head back to the service bar, grab all the liquor bottles you need, using all five arms that you have. Hopefully the girls all have their glasses properly set up, and you begin pouring. While you are pouring, you sort out which waitress ordered which drinks, in your head, so you can ring them on their tab. The girls are all shoving tabs in your face. You think okay, Debbie had the two Millers, one Manhattan, and one Dewar's and water. You push all the appropriate buttons so the computer-slash-cash register can ring it on their tab. Cathy had the Budweiser, the Piesporter, and the Smirnoff martini. Go, magic fingers, go! It's always a nice little ego trip when you can ring in drinks faster than the cash register can print everything, and you have to slide the tab in and wait for the register to catch up and print it out on the tab. Hey, you get your perks where you can! Now, before you get sidetracked, there are still two more girls waiting to have their drinks rung up on their tabs. (Actually, ringing drinks on tabs is an archaic activity that will soon be a thing of the past.)

In the middle of this flurry of activity, three more people sit down at the bar, so while the next batch of waitresses is at the service bar setting up their glasses, I run over to wait on the people sitting at the bar. While down at the other end of the bar, four patrons who have been there for a while decide it's time to eat. I give the four of them two menus and tell them to share, run back to the girls at the service bar, get them taken care of, run back to the other end to get the dinner orders. Two more people just sat down at the bar. Another waitress is at the service bar, wanting blended drinks of all things!

"What the fuck!?!?! What idiot ordered ice cream drinks?!?!

Did you tell them this was gonna ruin their appetite?!?! This is a real time waster!" I start unwrapping two little squares of ice cream, throw them in the blender. Oops, there was still a little piece of wrapper stuck to the ice cream. Oh well, a little fiber never hurt anyone. Add a shit load of booze (wimps usually order ice cream drinks, so if you make it strong enough, they won't order another), some ice, and turn on the super charged blender with the diesel engine. This thing could grind glass or even silverware.

I pour the concoction into a pain-in-the-ass-to-carry, long-stemmed tulip glass, top if off with whipped cream, and pour what extra there is into a little glass and slide the extra over to the guy sitting in front of me; he's a regular. The guy sitting next to him pipes in with a whiney "Hey, why don't I ever get to sample the leftovers?"

"Because I don't like you." Don't ever ask me a question you don't really want an answer to.

Two couples standing by the front door flag me down so they can have a drink while they are waiting for a table. Bob, who is standing behind where his two friends are seated, shouts, "Hey! I need another drink!" I shout back, "Hey! What's wrong with the one in front of you!?!" Bob opens his mouth as he glanced down at the bar and finally noticed that his drink had already been refilled. Do you really have to wonder why we develop "attitude?" (Of course, for some of us, attitude isn't something you just develop with time; it's a gift.) I sped off before Bob could answer. Two more waitresses are at the service bar. Refills are needed for the four who ordered dinner. The two right in front of me want soup. Another guy sits at the bar. It's Friday. It's now wall to wall people. All the seats are filled. Those standing behind them all want drinks. The cook is shouting that my dinners for the four are up, come get them before they get cold. The waitresses are ordering more drinks. The two couples at the front want another round to take to the table with them...

Ten minutes have gone by. Repeat this process over and over again for the next five and a half hours, non-stop. Don't panic, don't lose your temper, don't shoot anybody, don't lose your sense of humor, learn all of the short cuts you can, and oh yeah, have a good time. Fuckin'aaaa.

ASSIGNED SEATING

You may be asking yourself, just as Mach did, "There's no such thing as assigned seating at a bar, is there?"

The answer is "Yes."

If it's a crowded Friday night, and you want a seat, you have to wait until I tell you where to sit, which will get you a seat faster than if you tried to maneuver on your own. (Trust me. You're not that good) When you walk in, you're looking at full bar. I'm looking at a shift change for the customers. There are times when I have to prompt this shift change along. "Fred! You better hurry up and get out of here before your wife calls!"

"Oh shit! I'm gonna miss dinner. Gotta go!"

Works every time! Now I've got an empty seat.

P.S. Fred's wife has NEVER called.

We have protocol to follow here. And yes, it's my protocol, but it's fair and it works. I know who wants to sit with whom, who may still be coming in and their ETA, who got there first, who's staying, who's leaving, who's waiting for so-and-so to join them, and how many extra bar stools we can squeeze in. There's more to being a Bar Wench then just pouring drinks pretending to listen to people all night. Here's how the seating thing works.

The bar is "L" shaped, and it rounds out a little at the corner of the "L". The Friday Night Supper Club likes to sit at the curved part of the "L," so they can see each other and talk, which would be more difficult if they were all sitting in a straight line.

I need to point out that this is one of your better trained bar crowds, and the Friday Night Supper Club is working on their Masters Degrees in Seatology. As with becoming a master of anything, this takes years of patience and practice, but they learned the tricks. ("OH LOOK!!! Flying monkeys!" They will all turn their heads in unison.)

If they were waiting for another couple to arrive, instead of moving in empty bar stools so the newcomers would have a seat when they got there, they would instead spread out their seats a little and make it look full. You see, if they were to put empty seats there, by all rights anyone could claim them because we don't reserve seats at the bar. It's strictly first come, first serve. But where there's a rule, there's a way around it. So, by spreading out the stools, there is no empty seat to the untrained eye, but as the rest of the Friday Night Supper Club comes wandering in, they will notice that there are slight gaps, and go stand there. Upon their arrival, I will walk to the front, (about eight feet from the bar), where we keep extra bar stools for those waiting for tables, and snag a couple of them and drag them over to the bar. The spread out stools will now be pushed closer to each other, so we can fill in the gaps. It's a tight fit, but no one cares, because THEY have a seat. It's such a tight fit that I always tell everyone to use the restroom before they sit down "'Cause getting out ain't gonna be easy."

This group became so well trained that the first ones there would automatically spread out the chairs without me having to tell them to do it. They were happy, I was proud.

We had one couple that liked to sit at a precise spot in the middle of the bar, lined up right in front of the beer taps. They would trade seats as many times as it took, and then would inch their chairs over so they could get their exact spot. I found this to be too anal, so I decided they were on their own. I do my best to make sure everyone gets to sit, but if the bar stool is six inches too far to the right; I feel this is something that they can live with. When it came to them, I thought wrong.

We let this behavior continue (for years) because it became nightly amusement for the rest of the crowd and good betting fodder. How far would they go to get the "Exact Spot?" If someone next to them would leave, they would slide their bar stools over the requisite four to five inches to get right in front of the beer taps. My hypothesis is maybe Gladys had a radio hidden in her beehive hairdo, and she got better reception from the reflection of the shiny metal of the beer taps. OR…maybe they were wearing magnets and needed the metal of the beer taps to hold them upright as they stared to drift off and lean too far over to the side. (Okay, you come up with a better one.) What was that you said? They're aliens? We'll have a group discussion after Jeopardy!

As Mach walked in, in wide eyed wonder, (We TOLD him it was going to be crowded) he did as he was told and immediately tried to catch my eye. I already saw him and handed him his beer as he was about to open his mouth. I was my usual cheerful self, "Mach, go stand behind the guy wearing the rug. He's cashed out and ready to go." Oh c'mon, the rug thing was very obvious. Mach knew exactly who I was talking about. Well, actually everyone at the bar calls him that, "The Rug." Mach did as he was told. The Rug reached to pick up his keys off of the bar, swung one leg off the bar stool, and as soon as his foot touched the floor, Mach moved in. He slid a little too fast and bumped into The Rug, but he made a nice recovery and said that the lady on the other side of him had turned around and bumped into him. "I wasn't trying to rush you," he told The Rug and The Rug replied, "Don't worry about it."

Nice move, Mach. As the night moved on, and Mach observed the "seating system," he had to be a little impressed. I was a little impressed with Mach.

The Friday Night Supper Club, which consists of anywhere from three to seven couples, started filtering in. As if she'd been doing it for thirty years (instead of just ten). Linda made a bee line for the bend in the "L" when she saw one couple get up and leave, and spread out a few of the bar stools. She impatiently gestured for Jim, her husband, to get the lead out and scurry over and sit down before someone else slid there ass in there. A few minutes later, Noreen and Arnie came in, and followed the same procedure. Arnie pulled up next to Jim, and Noreen sat on the far side of Linda. These people had all been married FOREVER and felt no need to sit next to each other. They came here to talk to other people.

As I set down Arnie's drink, he looks up and says, "Dammit, I forgot the rules again! Make my next drink a vodka and tonic. I forgot to tell you I was switching." We have a rule here about switching drinks. You MUST tell me BEFORE you pass the service bar on your way in. If you are such a moron that you can't remember that you're going to switch drinks, and then it can hardly be my fault if I make you your usual.

Next to arrive is Art and Anna. There is room for another chair at the women's end of the group, so I scurry (yes, I scurry) to the front and grab it for Anna. Art decides to hang by the guys and shoot the bull. (Like he has any choice). Everybody's happy, including me. Most of us want to keep it that way. Once they start talking about food, everyone except Noreen, that is, Linda runs up to the hostess station and snags a few menus. Like she always says, "Why bother the Bar Wench when I can get them myself?" Then, Bob, the well dressed chef, comes out and tells Jim what fish special he came up with for the evening, so Jim really doesn't need a menu.

Alas, here comes couple number four: Dave, the one who wasn't buying into the petition signing gig for Nancy's Nachos, and Betty. Always happy to be here on Friday night, Betty and I exchange parade waves and air kisses, and Dave basically ignores us. He does however give a jovial greeting to the rest of the crowd. At this point in time, all seats are taken, but Dave and Betty are used to this, and social butterflies that they are, just wander at will and talk with everyone.

We haven't forgotten about Mach, he's chatting with some of the people still left from the afternoon crowd. I'm going to have to start dropping hints that their shift is over and it's time to turn over the seat to someone else.

As two of Mach's fellow conversationalists get ready to leave, I give Dave and Betty the "Hop to" sign; that's two quick nods to the right, and they vulture right in and end up next to Mach. As I set down another beer in front of Mach, I quickly introduce him to Dave and Betty, and tell them that he's foreigner, and they should be nice.

Betty leans over in front of Dave and says very slowly, yet with volume, "Hi, Mach, where are you from?"

Mach answers, "I'm not a foreigner. I'm from Boston."

Betty looks at him quizzically and says, "But you've got an

accent, and where did you get that name from? Is it an old family name, or is it Mach, like in Mustang?"

Mach carefully eyes Dave and Betty and asks, "Do you two know Helen? And I DON'T have an accent!"

"Well, yeah," Dave answers, "Everyone knows Helen. Why do you ask?"

"I think I had this same conversation last night. My name isn't Mach. It's Mach."

"OOHHHH!" A light goes on in Dave's eyes. "He's not saying Mach; he's saying his name is Mark."

Mach showed relief as he reached out to shake Dave's hand. "You're the first one who got it right. It's MACH."

Betty had to intervene, "Well, Mark, you're not doing a very good job of pronouncing Mark! It still sounds like you're saying Mach, like in Mustang."

"Why does everyone keep comparing my name to a car? Am I in the Twilight Zone or Purgatory?"

Dave kindly explained, "Look around ya, pal, ninety percent of the people in here work for the auto industry in one way or another, whether it's in one of the plants, or a small shop that supplies the plants, or a restaurant that's by some of the plants. It all goes back to cars. So what do you do, Mach? What brings you to this area?" Mach, Dave, and Betty are conversing, the Friday Night Supper Club is hip deep in conversation about absolutely nothing, others are shouting out answers to "Wheel of Fortune," and Ol' Mr. Bob has just left the bar and is at his table ordering dinner, (he has dinner here every night). Ol' Mr. Bob is in his eighties, knows everyone, has achieved celebrity status, and out of respect, NO ONE crowds in on Ol' Mr. Bob as he is vacating his bar stool. As he was getting ready to get up, Ol' Mr. Bob, being nobody's fool, spots Helen walk in the back door, waits for her to walk in his direction, and gallantly gestures for her to have a seat, and Helen accepts in an overly gracious manner.

Anyone still standing can't argue, after all. The kindly old gentleman gave the lady a seat. We're not complete heathens. Ol' Bob is slick, and Helen spits nails. Whose gonna argue? I'm not.

This is usually the time of the night when the group gets organized for "The Marge bet." They all try to figure out at what time it will get so busy that Marge has to use her famous Friday night line with the cooks. Dave and Betty holding are the pot for this one. After seeing several people slide a dollar down the bar and pick a fifteen minute time slot, Mach gets curious. He asks Dave, "Who is this Marge and what the hell are you betting on?"

Dave explains, "You see, Mach, every Friday when it gets busy and all the waitri are in a panic to get their orders, it's inevitable that sooner or later you'll hear Marge yell out, 'Who do I gotta blow to get some food around here?!?!?!'"

Mach innocently asked, "Does all activity in the kitchen stop as all the cooks try to be first in line?"

Dave took a deep breath and calmly replied, "I can see you haven't met Marge yet. How sad."

Mach was really curious now. "Is she here? Which one is

she?" He was starting to sound a little anxious. "Do I want to try and get in line with the cooks? Do you get in line with the cooks?" Dave slowly shook his head from side to side. As he saw Marge coming around a corner on two wheels, (some of the guys described her as Bigfoot, the truck, on steroids, with a bad perm and dye job and eyebrows that have to be trimmed with a weed whacker) Mach did a sudden and serious intake of breath and audibly gasped. Because Dave had pointed her out while Mach was in mid-swallow, the sudden intake of breath made Mach choke on his beer.

Good job Dave, I wonder if Mach will have the hiccups now. I hope so, I just love giving people my not-yet- patented hiccup cure.

I'm sorry, what? You want to know what the hiccup cure is? Okay, I can tell you, but then I have to kill you. Ready? If you really don't want to know, then just fast forward until I'm done talking. Here we go........You take a nice little hunk of lime and drop it into a rock glass, Pour some Angostura Bitters over the lime, stir a little, then sprinkle some salt over it, and stir again. Offer the lime on a cocktail sword (that always makes it so special) with the rock glass on the side. Dictate strict instructions to bite the lime twice and then spit it into the rock glass. The taste is so horrible; one usually has some sort of gag reflex action going on. This in turn totally takes their mind off the fact that until this point they had the hiccups.

One thing a bartender must always remember, you have

everything the customer and most of mankind wants: alcohol and food, the basics of life. Especially the alcohol. In order for the patrons to receive the quickest possible service, one must start to train the regulars to do things that help to expedite this process.

"Hey, Bob (it doesn't matter which one)! Reach in front of you, light one of my cigarettes, and set it in the ashtray!"

"Hey, Bonnie wipe up the bar in front of Bob while he's lighting one of my cigarettes!" As I throw her a neatly folded, damp towel.

"Hey, Danny put your empty plates in that bus tub over there!"

When it's this crowded, and you never stop moving, most people just do as you ask when you bark orders at them. Everyone wants to feel like they belong! They are rewarded when you set that next beverage down and they didn't even have to ask, (like Bob), and I am rewarded with respect, such as from those sitting around Bob, who took note to pay more attention than he did.

Suddenly we heard a "group moan," from the kitchen.

"Okay," Dave shouts, "Let's see who had 6:45 to 7:00 p.m."

Mach looked at Dave in a questioning manner. Dave lowered his eyes to the little piece of paper in his hand.

"AAAHHHH........" a light went off in Mach's head, "The bet."

"Uh-huh."

TOOLS OF THE TRADE

Since we are dissecting Friday night, let me explain some of the tools, weapons, gadgets and whatnots that we employ in the field of bartending. We've already seen some examples of how the customer can be used as a tool; now let's move on to some actual implements. This is a collection of inanimate objects that are probably more aware that they are being used than some of the customers.

Every occupation has its tools. In some circumstances, like the cavemen, you have to make do with what's at hand. They made their own tools out of rocks and sticks. That was very creative. As a bartender, all of the tools I needed were supplied for me. Some I would occasionally use (such as the menu) in a matter other than what they were intended for. That too, was very creative. For the terminally obtuse, I hit them with rocks and sticks.

THE COMPUTER

"HEY!" one of the Bob's yelled, "What's this little scrap of paper you just set down in front of me?!?"

"It's your tab."

"No, it's not! It's just a scrap of paper. A tab is larger, has writing on it, and I can read it!"

"We just got a new computer, and when I start a new tab, it prints out that little paper with a customer number on it. I can also give it a name if I want to type it in."

Well, what happens if I accidentally lose this little scrap of paper?"

"Nothing, I can still find it in the computer. You can eat it if you want to. But if you do that, I'll have to charge you for an appetizer."

How cool! We no longer had to add up the tabs using (of all things) simple arithmetic. All one had to do was type in a customer number and presto! A little piece of paper came sprinting out of the computer with an instant answer. Although, it wasn't as much fun as when one would ask, "Hey, how much is my tab so far?"

"Hey, yourself! It's sitting right in front of you Pick it up and do the math. You're a high school graduate."

"Yeah, well, how do you know?"

"Don't push it. We're giving you the benefit of the doubt."

I no longer had to cash out the waitresses or ring in their drink orders, or even talk to them, for that matter. When they needed drinks, a small printer would belch out yet another piece of paper, and their drink order would be neatly printed on it (as opposed to most of our gnarly handwriting), and I could have it ready by the time they walked over to the service bar. Or not. So now, instead of having to ring in their drink orders on their tab, as described in an earlier part of this chapter, I had more time to converse with my customers. Or not.

Time and steps were also saved by not having to walk the ten or fifteen feet to the kitchen to turn in my food orders. The computer sent them to the cooks on their cute little printer that in turn would defiantly spit out the same obnoxious little pieces of paper that were received behind the bar.

The computer at the bar would assign a number to each new tab that was started. We would then give each tab a name, so as not to get them mixed up. I don't recall any rule saying that you had to give each tab the actual name of the person to whom it was designated, so I took this as clue to get creative. When one of the Bob's asked for his tab and saw that it said "Little Bobby Butthead," he felt he had to comment.

"You know, I can stay home if I want to take this kind of abuse!"

"So, what's your point?"

"Uuummm, aahhhh.......uhhhhh......never mind."

One older gentleman was questioning the need for a costly computer system. I was explaining to him how much time was saved.

"You see, by not ringing out the girls tabs and making change when their table wants to cash out, or having to ring the drinks on them, it saves a few seconds here, a few seconds there...."

"But," he interjected, thinking it wasn't necessary to let me ramble on, "throughout the course of the night, do a few seconds really matter to justify the cost?"

"Well, it's just that. I don't have to run back to the kitchen to turn in the food orders; no one has to worry about making a mistake when adding up a tab…"

"Again," he asked, "do a few seconds really matter that much?"

"I can get you your drink faster."

Then his face lit up. "Aha! Why didn't you say so in the first place? Computers are a wonderful invention!"

THE MENU
(The actual menu itself, not the contents)

Since hitting people over the head with rocks and sticks is frowned upon nowadays, except for the severely obtuse (as was earlier mentioned), by the boss, among other people, I had to find a tool that would be effective, yet not leave a mark or do any great harm. Thus, I turned to the menu, as you have already seen with Mach and Vern.

The menu is a multi-purpose tool. It has its obvious uses, such as being a great display for the food items that are available and also being a wonderful placard upon which we can attach little papers that list the daily specials. Believe me, if we had to TELL you what the daily specials were, you would probably only get a partial list from any one waitress, and the list would be different with each one.

As you've already seen, menus also make a great whacking tool. I've used them for years as that. When someone says something incredibly stupid, and this happens on a daily basis, I found the menu was the perfect tool for hitting them upside the head. They're laminated, thus giving them the right amount of flex, so they don't tear. Some patrons became so well trained, (like Vern) that when they see me coming, they just lean their head forward and take their punishment.

Of course, there are times when a surprise attack is needed. In these circumstances, I would point out the offender to one of the more cooperative waitri, (that's the Latin plural for waitress), or Helen, and then either she or the waitri would walk by with a menu and whack them from behind. Things always run so much smoother when you and your fellow employees can work as a team. Let me add that Helen may occasionally tell someone where to sit, or where to go for that matter, thus making her an honorary employee. We actually didn't have any choice in this matter. Helen TOLD US she was going to be an honorary employee. As she pointed out to us, she puts in more hours then some of the real employees. I didn't have a problem with this. It's nice to have back-up.

We can also help you make a decision when you are perusing the menu and trying to decide between a couple different entrees. When you ask, "How's the lasagna tonight?" You may hear, "It's great, but you should be on a diet. What's your next choice?"

Be careful how you respond to this, you may get hit with menu.

ALCOHOL

You may not think this is a tool, but when you put the customer in the right frame of mind, it's the most powerful weapon behind the bar. Oh, I know what you're thinking. It's my job to serve drinks. Well, yes it is, but one also has to keep a lid on the crowd so no one gets too unruly.

SO…when someone says something to really piss me off, I tell them, "Why you want to mess with the person who has all the alcohol is beyond me." Yes, I know I already said this; I'm just trying to see if you're paying attention.

Some catch on right away; others have to ponder this statement for a moment. They may declare that I HAVE TO serve them, and they would be right. To a certain extent. We do have the right to refuse service to any at any time, as along as it is not discriminatory. Keep in mind, I don't discriminate, I pick on everyone!

So let's say some Bozo decides to complain that his drink is too weak… "Hey! Did you put any whiskey in here? I can't even taste it!!!"

"Maybe you're just a lush." Yada….yada…yada. Do ya really think that the owner is gonna tell me to pour heavier???? He's the one who has to pay for that liquor! He certainly isn't in business to give it all away! Besides, he doesn't like you either.

As easy rule of thumb to remember is: When you are the one drinking, you DO NOT hold the trump card (actually, you weren't even dealt a hand), and you probably don't hold your alcohols as well as you think you do. Before you decide to spew forth such witticisms as "The customer is always right," which people only use when they have nothing else to say (this will be discussed more in depth later), or "Money talks and bullshit walks," you might want to check and see if you've got comfortable shoes on. If you really want to push it, pull out all of your money and try to make it talk. You're still gonna walk.

WALKER FOR THE AGING WAITRESS

I know this may sound rude, but why should one have to give up the work they love just because they can't get around as well as they used to? This implement hasn't actually been built yet, but I've got the blueprints, and I'm sure it would be a big hit. Younger waitri may even be jealous. And we all know that there are some older waitri who could still take better care of a table at 105 years old than some young airhead who can't spell toast.

Alright, back to the WAW. (Figure it out.) First of all, it would have wheels. I think this is an obvious necessity. One does want the food on the plate when it arrives at the table, so wheels would do away with the clump, clump, clump when walking to the table. It would also have hand brakes, one on each side to avoid going in circles. And of course, the tray rack across the top. I have just described the basic model. Now let's get into the options!

First, we'll start with the condiment holders. They can be attached either to the front of the walker, or along the sides, depending upon how many are desired. These can hold anything from ketchup and mustard to fresh parmesan and a pepper mill.

The next option is sure to impress your customers! How about a built-in microwave!!! This is especially handy for those tables in the far corners of the restaurant. This also comes with a complimentary oven mitt, for pulling those hot plates out of the microwave. A less expensive option for insuring the food remains somewhat hot on your trek to the table is a pizza delivery bag. Just lay it on the tray rack and stuff the plates in there. It'll work. Sort of.

For the safety conscious, and those working under OSHA rules, we can also install turn signals, or the flashing-light-on-the-pole assembly, which connects to the right front corner. Full height is approximately six feet high, AND...who can resist the sound package that makes that annoying BEEP BEEP BEEP noise you hear when commercial vehicles back up?

I know there's someone out there waiting to shout, "What about the helmet?" Welllll...if you're still waiting tables and need the WAW, then you know ALL the tricks of creating your own hair spray helmet, so wearing another helmet would just be redundant.

OH! One final option I need to mention is the "battering ram." This is for those busy nights when you are speeding through a crowded restaurant and some inconsiderate, oblivious baboon is blocking the aisle, and when you shout "Excuse me!" and he just gives you a cursory glance. With the flick of a button, the baseball bat battering ram swings out and hits him in the knees. Heh, heh, heh, this one always makes me smile.

THE GLARE

I was driving along with my son one day, and he said something that caused me to glance in his direction. Then he innocently asked me, "How do you do that?"

I inquired in return, "How do I do what?"

    a) "How do you get that look on your face that says 'Shut up or die?'"

"OOOHHHH… That look. It's a gift, it's a mom thing." (Heh-heh)

This also works on bar patrons. You can melt them right down into their bar stools. It's a great mind-fuck. As soon as you give them the "Glare," which any woman who is still breathing can do, it tells the recipient one of two things: "You are WAY TOO stupid to even talk to," or it triggers something in their mind that sends them back in time to when they were eight years old and this "Glare" became indelibly etched in their brains from encountering this look on a weekly basis. The immediate reaction is a cringe, followed by a split second tensing of every muscle in the victim's body as he waits for the punishment.

Of course, no physical punishment is forthcoming. Well, maybe a menu whack. Never give them a menu spank. They like it too much. Oftentimes, they will just quietly sit for a while, shaking off past ghosts, still not sure what just happened to them.

To really drive a point home, or to make the slightly paranoid even more so, every now and then, I just look at them. Head gently tilted, one eyebrow raised, and lips a little snarly.

They're not sure what they did, but resolve to never do it again.

TIME OUT

Time out isn't just for kids. Here's an example.

On any given evening, Bob (it doesn't matter which one) makes an incredibly ignorant comment, like "I liked the outfit you wore yesterday better."

WHOOAAAHH!!! The correct way to verbalize those thoughts would be, "You look stunning tonight, as usual; however, the color of yesterday's outfit was exceptionally complimentary to your eyes."

The lesson here for everyone is: Bob (It doesn't matter which one) speaks without thinking, again. So now, Bob has to pay the price. As soon the words stumble out of his mouth, those sitting around him quietly moan and start to inch their chairs away from him, or at the very least, face the opposite direction. They know what is coming. Bob looks a deer in the headlights wearing a blond wig. Bob is going to get put in "Time Out." Again. The procedure for "Time Out" is simple; no one is to talk to Bob for ten minutes, unless they too want to suffer the consequences. As Bob, looking like a dejected child, helplessly peers around, the rest of the crowd just shrugs their shoulders at him or ignore him altogether. Since the ten minutes that Bob will be in "Time Out" will seem endless to him, the others only have but minutes to place their bets (there is no end to the betting) as to who will wander over and try to engage Bob in a conversation. Bob has to answer in order to win the bet. BUT, Bob knows that there will be an extension of his "Time Out" minutes should he speak. (You didn't think the bet was gonna that easy, did you?)

Dave and Betty have bet on the next person who walks in the back door. It's a wide open choice, the next person who walks in may not even know Bob, but I guess that's why they call it betting. It's all a game of chance. They're hoping Bob will forget his current situation when someone walks in and says "Hi, Bob. How's it going?" It's happened before.

Bob (a different one) and Darlene have chosen Daisy, the Never-gonna-be-a-Rhodes-Scholar waitress. Daisy hears the words "Time Out," associates it with a break, and usually goes outside to have a cigarette. The chances of her sashaying over and asking Bob if he would like to join her outside for a cigarette are very good. Of course, Bob would be deeply flattered that a pretty girl asked him to join her for a smoke, but again, he must remember his situation.

Then, there're always the cheesy bets. You know, the ones who bet on themselves thinking they can get Bob to talk. These are usually the same people who at one time or another have ended up in "Time Out" also.

The Boss happens to come around the corner, sees Bob looking like an island among the sea of patrons, looks at me, I nod towards Jim, (he's holding the money), and he wanders over and puts his money on Bob the Well Dressed Chef.

The next person in the back door is one of the truck

drivers. He gives his group greeting to all at the bar as he makes his way back to the truckers table. Bob passes the test. Not even so much as a nod. All are impressed with his self control, but it knocks Dave and Betty out of the race.

After the truck driver, Vern walks in. Being a veteran of many bar bets, Vern immediately knows what what's going on the second he walks in the door.

"Hi, Bob said something stupid again, huh?"

The crowd all murmurs "Uh-huh," and nods their heads in unison.

"Is it too late to get in on the bet?"

Jim, tonight's keeper of the scorecard and cash, tells him there's only six minutes left, but if he wants to get in, that's okay.

Vern asks if anyone has chosen Monica, finds out no one has, and throws in his money.

The pot is up to eight dollars now.

The next thing we know, Monica is swooping down on Bob and whispering in his ear. Immediately everyone knows that Vern must have cut a deal with Monica. (Vern works real fast.) If she can get him to talk, he'll split the pot with her. However, her attempt fails, as all she managed to do with whatever she whispered was to get Bob to turn a really deep shade of red out of embarrassment.

Another minute elapses; those who bet on themselves are making clumsy attempts with asinine chatter to get Bob to break. What they don't realize is that the three of them are throwing out comments so fast that Bob doesn't have time to process ANYTHNG they are saying. It's all just a blur.

With a minute and a half left, Bob the Well Dressed Chef appears behind the end of the bar and shouts over to the Bob who is in "Time Out," and asks, "Hey, Bob, how do you want that T-bone cooked?" A completely startled Bob, with eyes and mouth wide open, sits bolt upright in his seat and quickly shouts back, "I DIDN'T ORDER A STEA..." as he realized his error. His desire not to speak, lest he suffer further punishment, was overcome by his fear of having to pay for a meal he didn't order.

"Bob, you idiot. You fell for that again!"

The Boss wandered over, picked up his winnings, and split them with Bob the Well Dressed Chef.

We let Bob who was in "Time Out" slide on the rest of his sentence, but only because he had inadvertently provided us with much entertainment. Don't feel bad for Bob. If he didn't get put in "Time Out," he would never in a million years get this much attention.

THE REMOTE CONTROL FOR THE TELEVISION(S)

As at home, he who has the remote rules. BUT...if you are lucky enough to have the remote firmly clenched in your greasy little popcorn grabbing palm (oh yeah, we have free popcorn for everyone who wants it, unless we burn it, and then no one wants it), then you will be the subject of severe ridicule should you make an error in your choice of programming. (Everything at the bar has its price.) Everyone is thrilled for you that your daughter made her high school's synchronized swimming team, but NO ONE wants to watch it on the local access channel. Programs depicting surgical procedures would be a bad choice if some are still eating their dinner. I, personally, do not wish to see nature shows about snakes and will remove the remote from your control should you leave on one of these programs for more than five to ten seconds. (You won't even know the remote is no longer in your greasy little popcorn-grabbing, face-stuffing palm until you try to change the channel Even then you may not notice). Since there are three televisions in the bar area, disputes as to what should be on are easily resolved. Majority or me rules, and that program is shown on the television directly behind the bar.

The next most popular choice is shown on the television that is to the left and back a little from the bar, so one has to sit at an angle. No big deal. The last program, oh forget about the last program, no on really cares anyway. There have been occasions when someone has borrowed the remote for the television in the dining room and neglected to return it. This is a very serious no-no. If it is not returned soon enough, those at the bar slowly start to turn into mouth-foaming rabid pit bulls, or develop a attitude similar to Helen's when she has PMS and is down to one pack of cigarettes Either way, it's not pretty.

Most of the time, we'll ask whoever is waiting on that table to fetch it for us (I know that sounds so rude, get over it, I have) and drop it off at the bar. Most waitri usually just throw it when within three feet of the bar and then run for fear of getting bitten of the arm. I wait for the pit bulls to all scramble after it, then I say, "Oh look! I found the extra remote!" (Heh-heh)

You may also lose remote control privileges for a number of other offenses. For instance, if you say something I find offensive, you will simultaneously be hit upside the head with a menu while the remote control is removed from your paw.

If you suffer from clicker madness and have an uncontrollable urge to change the station every tenth of a second, the rest of the crowd will not be forced to suffer with you. You will probably never be allowed to handle the remote control again. Ever.

If you are the new kid on the block, and the bar is filled with salty old regulars, you won't even have a vote for six months, much less be able to touch the remote. Seniority does have its benefits. Besides that, it just wouldn't be special if we let you have a turn right away.

WHEN EATING AT THE BAR....

THE ORDERING RITUAL

Many of the regular customers know that statements like "We're ready to order now!" will be met with a response not heard in most restaurants, such as "Good for you" as I keep walking to the other end of the bar. Or, "I don't see a cast on that arm, write it down yourself. And remember, spelling counts. If you are going to use abbreviations, make sure they are restaurant approved. If I can't understand it, you won't get it."

Or, there's always the ever-so-popular line, "We've decided!"

"Okay, it's about time. You've been studying the menu for so long you should have imprints of it on your corneas, the kitchen is ready to close, and we're out of most of the specials. Maybe you should go take a remedial reading course so you can speed up this process. Either that, or I can give you the picture menu next time."

Did I mention that spelling counts? If you can't spell it, you can't eat it. Occasionally there are spelling errors on the special cards, which are written up daily. One night broccoli was one of the veggies, and it was misspelled on the special card. Betty was trying to order broccoli, but after seeing it misspelled, she was having a difficult time remembering the correct spelling. She wrote down "brocoli," then crossed it out, and changed it to "brocolii," and crossed that out, too. She was having a hard time remembering if there were two "c's," or two "l's, and finally wrote down "red skins," in what little room she had left.

Then there was the guy (who was a very regular patron), who misread the description of a particular chicken dish on the special card one evening. When his food arrived, he ranted and raved that that was NOT what he had ordered! I showed him the card again, but he was on a roll, and not ready to admit he screwed up. He said he would eat it anyway. Like he had any choice in that! It was either eat it or wear it, in which case he could receive the nutrients through osmosis, as it seeped in through his skin. I, personally, would find eating it more enjoyable.

The next day, before he ordered dinner, he did acquiesce that he had misread the special card the night before. He was quite sheepish about ordering his food for that evening. I asked him if he was SURE he knew what he was ordering. He quietly replied, "Yes, I'm sure. I read the menu thoroughly."

"GOOD! Because if you complain tonight I'm going to serve it to you suppository style!"

THE PLACE SETTING

Just because you're eating at the bar, doesn't mean you

can eat like an animal. You're sitting in front of a crowd, for crying out loud. They can all see you eating!

First of all, we're going to start out with the requisite place mat. I've had people tell me, "Oh, I don't need that." My standard reply is, "Yes, you do. I've seen you eat." That usually shuts them up, as they sit there with their mouth slightly agape. More than once, I've had to walk over and whisper, "Close your mouth. That look is really quite unbecoming." More than once, some unsuspecting fool has left his mouth hanging open a bit too long, only to be brought back to consciousness when he realizes people are trying to throw stuff in his mouth. Every now and then you can hear Vern say, "Aim for his eyes. Try to put his eye out!"

Most of the time you will get the standard restaurant silverware setting. One knife (not sharp), one spoon, and two forks. These utensils all come wrapped in a napkin. (How fancy!) It's a lot of fun to watch those with diminished motor skills, aka, the Happy Hour leftovers, have a really hard time just trying to unroll the napkin and not drop at least one utensil on the floor. The other day Vince was all proud and shit that he hadn't dropped any utensils, until he heard a crash and realized he had knocked an ash try on the floor.

Many a time someone has asked, "Which fork do I use first?" I always tell them to use the small fork first. Then I snicker to myself as we yet again see that ever so intelligent, mouth-slightly-open look as they sit there and compare the forks to see which one is smaller. They are all the same size. Next, they'll stand the forks up side by side, and when there is no obvious difference, they lean them over to look at them straight on. Morons. At this point, I just grab one and bark, "Start eating!"

Before they are finished with the salad, and the fork gets taken away, you can see them trying to sneak in one more comparison test. Fools.

BEVNAPS

You will ALWAYS have a bevnap under your drink. If it sticks to the glass, PULL IT OFF! We can always get you another one. Remember, (and this is very important), I DO NOT want to have to wipe the bar off under your glass every five minutes, so USE YOUR BEVNAP! There are no rules that say you can't change it yourself. In fact, we encourage it.

There are some who pour salt on the bevnap, thinking they are clever, (not their first mistake).

"Look, now it doesn't stick!"

"Hey you moron you've got salt all over the bar!"

"But it doesn't stick!"

"That entire salt shaker is gonna stick someplace if you don't clean that up! I can't believe you poured salt all over the bar!" You have to know I'm still glaring at the moron. Someone has to know. The moron doesn't.

Back to my yelling "Do you want a damp towel to clean that up with?!?"

"But....."

"Or do you want to lick it off of the bar?"

For some reason, they always choose the towel. Dammit.

CONDIMENTS

I have the salt and peppers shakers on a shelf behind the bar, neatly lined up like little tin soldiers. Do you really want to break up the formation just because you want to over season your food?

I can hear it now…. "Can I have the salt, please?"

"NO, they put enough in there when they cooked it!"

"Well, then, may I have the pepper?" said in a more timid tone than the request for the salt.

"No, you're trying to quit." Most will ponder this statement about half way through the meal.

"May I have some mustard, please?"

"Not if you're going to put it on those french fries."

"May I have the condiment tray, please?"

"No, you're too clumsy. Last time you knocked it over."

"May I have some A-One Steak Sauce, please?"

"Not in this lifetime. We do not put ANY sauce on a filet."

"May I have some ketchup for my fries, please?"

"Yes, just don't use too much or I'll have to charge you extra."

"Can…"

"NO!"

"I dropped my napkin on the floor. May I have another,

please?"

"Those grow on tress, you know."

"Well, yeah, but I really need another one."

"If you had better table manners, you wouldn't."

"Pleeeeaaaaassssssseee....."

"Okay, but if drop this one, then I have to charge you for a third one."

"May I have a toothpick, please?"

"Well, of course you can! No one wants to look at all that dinner residue in your teeth. This is also your lucky day. Toothpicks are on special today! Usually they're a quarter a piece, but you can have three for a dollar!"

"Oh, okay, then I'll take three. HEY!!!! Wait a minute...."

"Works every fuckin' time."

I'm sorry if you think I'm too harsh. Well, no, I'm not, but really, these are just rules you will find in any household to keep some form of civilized behavior at the dinner table. And for God's sake, DON'T TALK WITH YOUR MOUTH FULL! Trust me on this one. You have absolutely nothing to say that could possibly be that important. Or of any importance at all, actually. Wait until you are through chewing, and (stay with me here) swallowing! Don't try to swallow too fast just because you can't wait to utter your inane comment. If you try to swallow too much or too fast and start to choke, all we're gonna do is throw you a bone. Literally. (Can't say you weren't warned.)

Around here, the Heimlich maneuver was something Bob

tried on a date, and that's why he walks funny.

Continuing onward.....

There are times when it is perfectly acceptable to make up your own food accompaniments. A food accompaniment is something you make from condiments. For example, we mix together sour cream and horse radish to get our horsey sauce for roast beef. Some people (actually very few) mix ketchup and mustard together for a french fry dipping sauce. We don't actually encourage this one. However, one food accompaniment that is quite popular (among the ten or twelve people that knew about it) is Secret Ranchero Sauce. Now, I'm going to let you in on a secret and reveal the recipe. The standard version of this delectable medley of mouth watering flavors is *$%7 @*(%%$)) and *$&%# with a little bit of &*$%^$>

HA!!! Did you really think I was going to give away a secret recipe?!?!?

Oh, I can hear you now. That's not fair! You said you....

Toughen up, kid, life's not fair.

ALRIGHT!!! Since I don't plan on bottling this stuff, I'll tell you the secret.

First of all, you need a soup cup or bowl. Don't use one of those shallow monkey dishes, or you'll slop the stuff all over the counter. Hey! I've seen how you handle forks and spoons, and I'm really glad there are no knives involved in this process. Back to the recipe.

Pour some ketchup into a bowl, and then add some ranch

dressing. Stir very thoroughly. If you have to ask what the exact quantities are, then you need to have someone else do this for you. If you want that added punch, then stir in some horse radish. To really kick it up, add some Tabasco Sauce.

What was that? You want to know what is dipped in Secret Ranchero Sauce? French fries, you idiot, what else would it be good for?"

DESSERT

"May we have some dessert, please?"

"I can't believe you have any room left for dessert after all you ate! What are you on? The 8000 calorie, gain six pounds a day, Sumo Wrestlers Diet?"

"Well, I was going to ask if you would like to split it with me."

"Split it with you!?! What kind of pig do you think I am?!? I'll just have a small bite or two. Oh, and I'll need a cup of coffee to go with that. It's over there. And, be quick about it! Go get it now. I want that coffee here by the time I bring out your dessert, or you won't get any of it."

There has to be some incentive to get them moving.

When I go out to eat, I'm usually so full from everything I've stuffed into my mouth I rarely order dessert. That's why this section is so short.

AFTER DINNER COFFEE

If you are one of those people who like an after dinner coffee, then there are rules that go along with that ritual also. Hey! I don't make up all these rules, I just enforce them! Well, yes, I do make them up, and then I bend the hell out of them. But they're good rules. So, anyway, whenever you feel ready for that coffee, just waddle on over to the coffee station and get yourself a cup. If you use cream in your coffee, those little creamer cups are over there too. And most important of all, be sure you ask me if I want a cup of coffee. Even if I have just finished half of someone else's dessert and already have a cup in front of me. It's not for you to decide if I need another cup. You have no ideas where my caffeine levels are, and you don't want them to get low. If you can't carry two cups and your stupid little creamer things, then you can put the creamer things in your pocket, or you can make two trips. It's not my fault you can't carry more than one thing in one hand at a time. This is a good rule because it allows me more time to spend with the rest of the customers, and we got rid of your sorry ass for a few more minutes.

La la la, Friday night moves along... The Friday Night Supper Club has written out their order, Noreen now just refers to the Veggie Nachos as "The Usual," not wanting to repeat the burning bevnap incident. I grab bundles of wrapped silverware and place mats, give them to Linda, and she sets out everyone's place setting, letting me know as she does so, "You know, I can just get the silverware and place mats myself next time. It'll save you a few steps." All patrons should have this attitude. I should have this attitude. Yeah Right! Not in this lifetime!

Dave is writing out his order and passes it over to Betty, so she can add her order. As he does so, he warns her once again to get it right, so there won't be any unnecessary delays due to unacceptable abbreviations and poor spelling. Betty just makes a snotty face-you know, like when you were nine years old, "Yada...yada...blow me..."

Mach closes up the menu, and Betty, still questioning his ancestry and speaking slowly, offers to help him write out his order. Dave just rolls his eyes back in his head.

Betty asks Mach, "What's your choice this evening? With her head tilted to the side while smiling ridiculously. Mach gave Betty a quizzical look, and Dave quickly interceded, "Betty's using her waitress voice again. She started drinking before we got here. I'll help you out." (Dave knows the restaurant business.)

Mach relaxes a little and tells Dave he was going to have a New York strip steak this evening.

Dave wrote down, N.Y. and asked "King size or Queen size? And be careful how you answer."

Mach answered, "King size." Dave let out an audible sigh. "How would you like that cooked, Mach?"

"Medium," Mach replied.

Dave then asked if he wanted soup, salad, or cole slaw.

Mach saw the soup selections for the night were clam chowder, chicken noodle, or French onion. He decided on the

French onion.

Dave asked "Do you want a cup or a bowl?"

Mach replied, "If a bowl comes with the meal, then I'll take a bowl."

"Do you want cheese melted over the top? It'll be extra."

"Sure, why not," Mach told him. (We're not done yet.) Okay, last question Mach, do you want potato or veggie? They're listed at the bottom of the special card.

"I guess I'll have the red skin potatoes with that."

I suddenly swooped in (Yes, I swooped, and it's very cool) and said "You guess?! Don't you know if you want the red skins or not? The man is trying to help you out!!! Tell him what you want!!!"

Just as suddenly, I darted away. Mach stopped holding his breath, and Dave said, "I've got it, Pal. You're covered.

As I swooped by again (I feel like one of those big birds that's swoops down on small rodents) and snatched up Mach's order, Dave whispered to the nearest member of the Friday Night Supper Club that Mach had ordered onion soup. They passed this info along the bar like they were third graders playing telephone. Mach didn't have a clue that anything was even going on.

The minutes quickly passed and out came Mach's bowl of French onion soup. As I gingerly set down the plate that the soup bowl was sitting on, I told him, "DO NOT TOUCH the bowl. It is VERY HOT. I cannot impress upon you how many morons do not heed that warning and touch the bowl anyways."

Mach picked up his soup spoon and gently moved some of

the melted cheese to the side. Enough steam rose up to give four women a facial. He decided not to touch the bowl. In fact, he decided not to touch it at all, and instead let it cool for a few minutes. Upon observing Mach, I got the feeling that he knew something was up. I could see his eyes darting to the right and then darting to the left, like a kid caught stealing candy, looking to see if anyone noticed. Again he turned his head to the right, the Friday Night Supper Club all turned their heads away as soon as he looked in their direction. He turned again, and this time they were all looking at him.

Before he could say anything, I was in front of him. I reached under the bar and pulled out (with a flourish) a tube of toothpaste and slapped in down on the bar. He looked up and down and up and down between the toothpaste and me, head bobbing back and forth like he was watching a tennis match on a very small court. "What on earth is that for?!?!" he asked.

I told him, "Just put a pinch in between your cheek and gum when you're through eating. Just because you want to eat onion soup doesn't mean the rest of us have to breath in the aftermath of onion soup every time you speak! The intoxicating aroma of onion soup is only pleasant BEFORE it is consumed."

Mach was a little stunned. He looked helplessly over at Dave, his new mentor and asked, "Does she give this to EVERYONE who has onion soup?"

Dave answered very matter-of-factly, "Everyone except Vern."

"Why doesn't Vern get the toothpaste? What makes him so special?" Mach demanded.

"It's not that Vern is special, it's just that last time he got the toothpaste, he used it to write his name on the bar. After that, he was forever banned from handling the toothpaste again."

"But what if he orders onion soup?"

"Oh, he's banned from that, too."

MORE FOOD ITEMS (NOT FOUND ON THE MENU)

The way to the wait staff's good side is through their stomach. (Well, actually that's second to leaving a big tip.). Think about it. Food is a pretty universal tool. It's been traded as currency, everybody needs it, everybody wants it, and since we (those of us working here) are on our feet, running around or five or six hours at a stretch, we can toss in a few extras morsels and not worry about it. (At least not until we get to be, umm, well, gee, fort...thir...older than we are now.)

If you occasionally bring in treats that are NOT available at the restaurant, you will be very popular. Sure, some may say it's a cheap trick, but if it gets you better service, wouldn't you try it?

I've got an old buddy who decided to go into the cheesecake business. He made cheesecakes and sold them to local restaurants. We, the waitri and I got to be the guinea pigs. You've never seen a happier group of guinea pigs.

Cake Man, (not his real name), would wander in the back door, set a cheesecake down on the service bar, and RUN! If I was busy and he didn't think I saw it right away, he would tell me it was there. This was totally unnecessary. We, again, the waitri and I can smell any food set on the service bar from the farthest section of the restaurant, even if it is wrapped in Saran Wrap and in a box.

One waitress was overheard to say at one of her tables, "Can you hurry up and order, please? There's a cheesecake with my name on it, and I don't want to have to get ugly."

The reason Cake Man would run is when we would approach the irresistible (it doesn't matter which flavor) cheesecake, with forks in hand, he likened us to a feeding frenzy of sharks. He was afraid of getting stabbed by an errant fork. How ridiculous! Chicken Shit! We are seasoned professionals! We have NEVER stabbed one another with a utensil or even gotten any of our forks locked together!! I know you're thinking that is preeeetttty amazing, considering the rate of speed at which we fly over with our forks and dig in. We consider it a gift. (Hey, everyone's got something.)

The real reason Cake Man brought in the cheesecake, was to get an honest critique of his cakes. One of the tests he uses is a time test. If the wait staff went to check on their tables and returned to the service bar before they had completely finished swallowing the previous mouthful, he knew he had a hit. You see, they were running back to get more before it was gone. (I told you we were quick) If no one hurried back, then he might want to go on to the next flavor.

As the waitri scurry by after their second mouthful (I say mouthful because bite just wouldn't be an accurate description of the cheek-bulging-serving-spoon-size piece of cheesecake that was being stuffed into any mouth on the run), he just made eye contact with them to get a nod or a thumbs up or any other positive sign. None of them could speak with that much food in their mouths. Nor would we want them to.

"What's that, Bob? NO, that's cheesecake making Carey's cheek bulge out. No…it's just…but…yes, I'm sure that she was NOT making her cheek bulge out by pressing her tongue against. Okay, that may be the international sign for blow job, but no, you are not going to get lucky."

PIZZA

Just about everyone likes pizza. (Or should, according to me). We were fortunate to have two customers who owned pizza places and possessed enough common sense that, on occasion, they would bring in a pizza or two for our (mostly my) enjoyment. (Hey! I still have the alcohol and you don't!) I always considered this a real plus since I LOVE pizza, and it was not on our menu. This usually occurred later on in the evening, well past the dinner hour. There were a few times when one of the regulars ordered something from the Nite Owl menu, and then they became dismayed when Vinnie strutted in the back door and set a couple of pizzas on the bar.

"If I had known you were having pizza, I wouldn't have

ordered anything."

"Well," I would tell him, "that's exactly why we didn't tell you." The boss frowns upon losing business to someone else, especially right in his own restaurant.

After the one who has ordered is served (we're not stupid), we call the boss, who's sleeping on the couch downstairs in the office, to come and have some pizza. It's kind of a Catch 22. He's going to yell if we call him or not. It's been a quiet night, so we call him. He's gonna come up and say, "What the hell??? Whatta you got there? What the hell? We don't serve pizza here!"

All the while, he's reaching for a piece. Then he looks over at me and says, "Whatta you let them do this for?!?"

"Here Boss, take this piece. It's got more stuff on it."

At this point, he pauses and grabs a second piece to take back to the office with him. He'll still be mumbling as he makes his way down the stairs. How can he yell at us when his mouth is full? He does make a futile attempt, just to keep up appearances. If we hadn't called him, he would've nagged us for the next week.

The food we serve is very good, but after eating off the same menu for ten or fifteen years, it is nice to a have something a little different. Obviously the boss thinks so too.

"Hey Bob! Get me a cup of coffee!" (It's not just for breakfast.)

MINI PASTRIES

AT Christmas time, one of our regular couples used to

bring in some mini pastries that were to die for (because that's what you'll do if you try and take mine). This was the greatest collection of sweets you have ever laid your eyes on. There were the cutest, most delicious looking mini napoleons, éclairs--I'm drooling just thinking about these, cream puffs, ooohhhh...and more. These pastries could almost make you wet.

The great thing about mini pastries is that you can sample a lot of different ones instead of just having one big éclair and being done with it. Or not. It wasn't unusual to see the wait staff walking around munching, again, on the way to one of their tables, trying to finish off one of these morsels before they actually had to speak.

There aren't any names on these pastries. This is a first come, first grab situation, so if there is anything in particular you want, you better be quick. And don't think you can grab one and set it down somewhere to save it for later. You won't find it where you set it. You'll look at the table and see someone walking away chewing.

At times like these, teamwork is essential. "Hey, you've got what I hope is whipped cream on your chin."

"Wipe that powdered sugar off of your nose."

"That cream puff in your apron pocket is starting to squish out."

"You're supposed to leave your cigarette in the ashtray when walking to your table."

LIQUOR CRITIQUE

One does get a chance to sample all the bottles behind the bar in a twenty-five year time span. After all, I feel I should be able to honestly critique what's in all those bottles. However, most people will drink what they want regardless of what anyone says. As you will see in the following Liquor Primer, no one really listens to my opinions. At all. Some even think my opinions are a bit strong and one sided. Oh well, to each his own, or in other words, numb your taste buds out in the manner of your choice.

I remember this one broad decided that MAYBE she would switch drinks. She seemed to take this decision as seriously as others do the decision to move. To another state. When asked what I would recommend, I glared back just a seriously and flatly said, "Beer."

"Ooohhhh," she pondered this thought. (Let's alert the media). "I hadn't thought about that. Would you suggest draft beer or bottled beer?" She really felt she was talking professional to professional here.

"I would go with the bottle beer."

Once again, she sat and pondered with at seriously

quizzical look on her face, which is not always a good thing, and asked, "Does bottle beer have a richer flavor than draft beer?"

"That would be an individual opinion in the world of draft beer versus bottle beer. I suggest the bottle beer because it's easier and quicker for me to serve," and with that quickly walked away to the imaginary emergency at the other end of the bar.

So much for rambling, let's move on.

"Hey, Bar Wench! What's your beverage of choice?"

"Well, let me start by saying thank you for asking and telling you what I don't drink!"

THE ALCOHOL PRIMER

GIN

As I was describing the taste of gin to someone, I likened it to distilled pine trees, with a little kerosene mixed in for that extra flavor boost.

I remember talking to a young attorney one time, who started drinking Beefeater's (gin) martinis, because he thought that sounded like something an attorney should drink. So he spent quite a while choking his way through God knows how many martinis before he finally acquired a taste for them. As a side note, I never was convinced that the attorney really acquired a "taste" for Beefeater martinis, I think he just numbed out his taste buds. My first clue was the fact that he made a face every time he took a sip.

My first thought was, "Why bother?" Frankly, I think gin stinks. I can't stand the taste of it. If given a choice, I think I'd rather smoke the pine tree and use the kerosene to light it.

You know, come to think of it, gin had a really good front man. Whoever did the P.R. for gin and made everyone think that martini's were cool did one hell of a marketing job because I can't think of any other reason anyone would drink the stuff.

They say gin comes from England. If you think about it, their food isn't any good either. Maybe the gin is to dull the taste buds before digging into a bowl of gruel.

SCOTCH

Like gin, they always say Scotch is an acquired taste. My dislike for Scotch isn't as great as my dislike for gin, but it is very close behind. In fact there is less than a percentage point of a difference. Why would anyone want to acquire a taste for something that tastes like an old, worn out wooden barrel? I don't even want to think about what the barrel was used for! What if it used to hold worms!?!?

OH!! And Scotch drinkers tend to be a little snobbish about their beverage of choice. The older the Scotch is, the more expensive it is. I think this is due to the aging process. (I figured out this all by myself one day.) Since wood is a porous material, the longer the liquid sits in the barrel, the more that nasty flavor has a chance to seep out. So, if you can afford the more expensive Scotch, the less the flavor gags you.

Since Scotch is from Scotland (that was a real no-brainer), I believe they drink it as a matter of national pride. That and I'm sure it's less expensive there, and it is probably a great compliment to haggis. I had even heard (more than once) that the old-timers, after developing an ulcer, would mix Scotch with milk, so it wouldn't burn when it hit their stomachs. Is that desperate or what?!?

Someone actually did order this once. I slowly poured milk into the Scotch. I had to MAKE myself pour it. I was 99% sure the milk was going to recoil and curdle the second it hit the Scotch. Nope. No curdled mess. It was just another abomination in the wide world of alcohol.

VODKA

They say vodka has no taste. I say this comes from the same people who already deadened their taste buds on the gin and Scotch.

I would say vodka has a LESS offensive flavor than gin or Scotch, but there is still an alcohol flavor there. I think one of the reasons it has less flavor, is some how the Russians found a way to make alcohol without using trees or peat moss, or whatever, and still got a drink with a kick.

If you think about it, when you get far enough north, there really isn't anything to use as a flavoring. Have you ever heard of "Fine Russian Cuisine?"

Vodka, having a much less repulsive flavor, has become a very versatile alcohol. It is mixed with juice more than any other alcohol. If you tried to mix Scotch with juice, well, I just don't think I could do that to the juice.

It was also the answer to making the gut-wrenching martini somewhat more palatable by making it with vodka, instead of gin, but still maintaining its "cool" status.

On a side note, I had one little old lady drinking straight vodka on the rocks one evening. When she approached the bar and informed me that her drink was on the weak side, this was one of the few times I was at a loss. "I don't know what to tell you ma'am, you're drinking straight vodka on the rocks. I can't make it any stronger."

I realized her friend was slightly embarrassed when I caught her trying to move to another table.

This woman was known for her drinking (NO shit!), and I knew some people who knew her, and when I related the story to them, they passed it along, and it soon made it's way through the entire congregation at her church. No one was surprised. They were just amazed that I was able to walk away without a scratch.

Okay, back to vodka... Oh screw it, let's move on.

RUM

Rum and Coke. Who, over the age of eleven, hasn't tried a rum and Coke? Oh, I have an idea, instead of a rum and Coke, let's have a Cuba Libre! Oh wow! You just ordered a rum and Coke with lime. How tropical. If you have any self esteem at all, you will ALWAYS order a rum and Coke with lime, and NEVER call it a Cuba Libre! Even if you've been considered cool for thirty-five years, you be become an instant and forever dork, if you say Cuba Libre. Rum has a distinct flavor. Distinctly what, I'm not sure. Oh, by the way, I don't like rum either. Have you ever tried Meyer's Rum? It looks like thinned out tar and tastes the same, only a little sweeter. Captain Morgan's is more palatable rum, which would explain its popularity. Either that, or people are enamored of the pirate.

And now, there are those wonderful flavored rums, like coconut. It's VERY dangerous!!!! It tastes so good, you don't even know you're drinking alcohol until you get up to go to the restroom, and you realize that your legs fell off. Watch out for the orange rum, too, different flavor, same effect.

Rum is also used in a great variety of supposedly tropical and/or refreshing fruity drinks. It is used in Daiquiris, Strawberry Daiquiris, Banana Daiquiris, Piña Coladas, and with any other fruit product found right here in Michigan (we're so close to the tropics) that you want to grind up in a blender. Please peel and/or remove pits or seeds first.

You never really see anyone drinking rum straight. Thank God. Although it can be clear, like gin or vodka, you'll never see anyone drinking a rum martini. Besides, I don't think any self-respecting bartender would mix one. It just doesn't exist. Maybe those guys in the Caribbean knew better than to drink the alcohol straight, unlike the Brits drinking straight gin, or the Russians throwing down shots of vodka, or the Scottish and their Scotch on the rocks, or however they manage to down that swill without tossing their cookies, or haggis. Or maybe…the Caribbeans just smoked too much pot.

Here's a helpful hint to all the teenagers who try to sneak some booze out of the house. Don't put rum in an empty cough syrup bottle. It will take on the flavor of the cough syrup that used to be in the bottle, perhaps causing you to think that you don't really need to mix it with that bottle of Coke you bought from the party store that will also sell you a plastic cup of ice on a Friday night before you go to a high school sports function. BIG MISTAKE!!!

WHISKEY

When watching an old Western movie, have you ever noticed how, when the cowboy swaggers up to the bar and tells the bartender to give him a shot of whiskey, he makes a face when he downs it? Well, that hasn't changed in a hundred years. The shot drinker puts the glass up to their lips, they toss down the whiskey, they throw their head back, and they shake their head a little. (I think this is a knee jerk reaction from the brain, saying, "I can't believe you just threw that rot gut down our throat.") The eyes are squeezed tightly shut for a couple of seconds, then the head returns to the normal angle, and then it's moved from side to side as "Whewwww" is uttered. Now tell me that was fun and refreshing. Now try and tell me that was fun and refreshing in a manner in which one might believe you. It can't be done. Save it for later.

When whiskey is mixed with sweet vermouth (the cousin to the dry vermouth used in the martini) and you toss in a maraschino cherry, you have a Manhattan. I find these to be slightly more palatable than a martini. Just slightly. If you are a novice drinker and think you should order one of these because it has a classy name, think again. Manhattan is just another name for a glass of booze. Again, if you are a novice drinker and drink one of these be sure and hold on to something (like a hand rail) when you attempt to get up. On the plus side, you'll save a lot of money because you won't need to buy another drink. Just be sure you have your designated driver lined up.

Who, again, over the age of eleven, hasn't tried a Whiskey Sour? It sounds like a grown up drink. That first sip tastes like lemonade…Oh my God!!!!! What is that after taste?!?!? It's worse than tomato juice mixed with grapefruit juice!

"What's that you said, Norm? You LIKE whiskey and water? Well, you eat liver too, so what's your point?"

TEQUILA

I feel that "Te kill ya" is an extremely accurate name for tequila. If you are a tequila drinker, then it doesn't matter what you feel, you lost all sense of feel for anything after the first twenty shots.

As you may have noticed I am not a big fan of any of the traditional liquors, and this one heads the list! This some of the worst shit man ever put in a bottle. And then, just to add insult to the injury you will incur when you drink this worse than diesel fuel liquid, some asshole put a worm in the bottle! I have no idea what the point in that is, except perhaps to make it even more unappealing. At least the worm died happy. Does the worm ever shit in the bottle?

Somewhere, sometime, some genius decided to make doing shots of tekillya a ritual. You need a lemon, a salt shaker, and of course, a shot of tekillya. You lick your hand and pour some salt on it. That's fun. Then you down the tekillya and either lick the salt and then suck on the lemon, or vice versa. The order of this ritual is a matter of debate, as if it was important.

Remember the whiskey drinkers who closed their eyes during the shot process? Well, the tekillya drinker's eyes do the opposite, and their eyes bulge out in a most unattractive manner. They can't close their eyes because they have to find the lemon and salt QUICKLY! It is important that they find these two accoutrements QUICKLY, lest they lose their dinner. As the whiskey drinker shakes his head and "Whews," after the shot, the tekillya drinker makes a few gagging noises and the entire body racks with spasms. Then, they try to claim it was from the lemon. Uh-huh. If what they really want are the spasms, I'd be more than happy to zap them with a tazer.

The only two tequila drinks that ever became popular (or palatable) both had songs written about them. Go figure. The first that comes to mind is "Tequila Sunrise." The drink, Tequila Sunrise, is tequila, orange juice, and grenadine, which is very sweet red syrup. Pour the tequila in the glass, add the orange juice, and then add the grenadine, and the red syrup sinks to the bottom. Myyy…how pretty. This drink could be as mellow as the song "Tequila Sunrise"--as long as you leave the tequila out.

And who hasn't heard of a Margarita? Or the "Margaritaville" song? Wasting away again in Margaritaville, looking for my lost shaker of salt?" (You didn't lose the salt shaker, I hid it on you. Heh-heh.) This can be a very refreshing and tasty drink since all the ingredients the tequila is mixed with really drown it out. The salt on the rim helps a lot, too. You know, if you wanted to kill two birds with one stone (thirst and hunger) I bet you could just rim the glass with crushed tortilla chips. Salsa on the side, please.

If you've never had tequila, and you feel you've eaten too much that day and want to purge your system of everything you've eaten, just have a shot of straight tequila, no lemon or salt, and you will probably need to run to the nearest restroom. If you want to get rid of everything you've eaten in the last week, have a "Prairie Fire." It's straight tequila with a bunch of Tabasco sauce.

Happy dieting.

BOURBON

Bourbon sucks, but the names sure are popular. I always thought of Bourbon as a cousin to whiskey, except with better names. Good ol' Jack Daniels, Old Grandad, Jim Beam…. Why are these all named after people? Some are even on a first name basis with these "guys." When such a person mentions Jack, they're not talking about playing cards, hitting' the road, or raising your car up.

Bourbon gets its name from Bourbon County, Kentucky.

So, did it start out as moonshine? How odd that this potent potable should be distilled in a state that still has dry counties. You still hear people order, "Gimme a shot of Jack!" pick up the glass, gulp, throw their head back, make a few facial contortions, and exhale loudly. It's a ritual. I'm not sure why, but my best guess would be that you just can't belt this stuff down straight without some involuntary muscle contractions trying to reach your gag reflexes before this liquid lightening assaults the delicate membranes of your esophagus, thus upsetting the balance of nature. But, go ahead, mix Bourbon with Coke, you'll be just fine. You'll never rust from the inside out. But…., should you up-chuck Bourbon and Coke down the side of your car, it will eat the paint off.

Bourbon is not a versatile liquor. It does not mix well with anything that could turn it into a frou-frou drink, but it can be substituted for whiskey in a Manhattan. For the most part, Bourbon would be considered a "man's drink." (Only if you don't puke.)

BENEDICTINE

Benedictine was created by the Benedictine Monks. It really was. Read the bottle. It's not popular at all, and there is a very good reason for this. It sucks. Big time! The only use anyone ever found for Benedictine was to mix it with brandy. They created B&B, which isn't too shabby. It's an expensive after-dinner liqueur. The only reason I mention Benedictine is to point out to people the little known fact that we've had the same bottle of it sitting on the back bar for over 20 years. It's that bad. The bottle even looks old. It would take a brillo pad dipped in acid to clean it.

OTHER STUFF

At this point, you're probably wondering if there is anything in the wonderful world of alcohol that I do like. Well, of course there is. I like all the stuff that doesn't have that nasty alcohol taste. Yeah, yeah, what a wimp, like I haven't heard that before. Remember, I'm still pouring the stuff, and you're not, so go ahead and say something stupid so you can get a short shot.

Distillers have really come a looooonnnngg way in the last 30 or 40 years. There are a ton of drinks that you can actually enjoy and not gag, start mixing plaids with stripes, or take a liking to barnyard animals because you incurred brain damage.

KAHLUA

Kahlua is a yummy coffee flavored liqueur. I think it tastes a lot like chocolate, and since I consider chocolate to be one of the main food groups, Kahlua is on my list. This is wonderful when mixed with coffee, Bailey's, or White Crème de Menthe, in which case you call it a "Girl Scout Cookie, because it tastes just like a Thin Mint cookie. How great is that!?!?! You can have a cocktail and not start gagging before you've even taken your first sip.

Kahlua and cream is very popular. OH! OH! One night this fool was sitting at a table and ordered a Kahlua and cream. So, that is exactly what I poured him. We also had a bottle of Café Lolita, a cheaper version of Kahlua, sitting on the bar, but I hadn't touched it in quite a while.

People would get snotty if they thought you poured them an imitation. (Even though Café Lolita is quite tasty.) So anyway, this fool sent his drink back, saying I poured him the cheap stuff. I hadn't. So I make him a new one, but only because he could see me from where he was sitting. Otherwise, it would have been the trusty "new glass trick." (We'll discuss this later.)

So he drinks the second one, and then when he orders another, he does the same thing! Jerk. So I send him the same one back and told the waitress I never touched the other bottle. He argues, sends it back again.

When he ordered a third, I told the waitress to tell him he was welcome to walk up to the bar and watch me pour it. He craned his head from the table, shouted for me to hold up the bottle so he could see it, gave me his okay (I'm so honored), and then I poured his drink.

A little while later when he got up to use the restroom, I told him, as he walked by, to do himself a favor the time he was in the liquor store, save a little money, and buy himself Café Lolita 'cause he can't tell the difference. I didn't know anyone could get their nose that far up in the air. And it's so not masculine for a man. Tsk tsk.

FRANGELICO

Many of your more expensive liqueurs (if it's spelled liqueur instead of liquor, it's gonna cost more) can be readily identified by their distinctive bottles. Frangelico, for instance, comes is the taller, slimmer version of the Mrs. Butterworth's bottle. It's supposed to be a monk.

If you read the label, it even tells how to drink this fine hazelnut flavored liqueur. The label suggests you can have it straight up, over ice, or in coffee. It's really quite tasty. It's also socially acceptable to mix it with Bailey's or Kahlua. For a really great treat, mix it with ice cream, a liqueur called Caramel, toss it in the blender with some ice, and it tastes just like butter pecan ice cream!! I'm not kidding!!!

SCHNAPPS

AAAHHHH...the wonderful world of Schnapps! Back when I started bartending, the only Schnapps we knew was good ol' Peppermint Schnapps. It was delicious! It was a far cry from all the rot gut discussed earlier in this chapter. If you chose to do a shot and belt it down, it was a little rough, but at least you got that "fresh, minty" aftertaste that made you feel like you just brushed your teeth. With Nyquil.

As time went on, many other flavors of schnapps began to pop up. One of the first flavors that became very popular was apple. This stuff was really good! One time, I poured some apple cider into a crock pot, added Apple Schnapps, and a coffee filter with cinnamon, nutmeg, and allspice in it, tied shut with some dental floss. (Sorry, no cheesecloth) Sometimes you just have to compromise), and threw it into the crock pot as my brew steeped. This was a great cold weather drink.

Now they use it to make an Appletini, among other things. And you'll soon find out how I feel about calling drinks "martinis," or using any form of the word, WHEN THEY'RE NOT!

For a great dessert drink, we would pour some Apple Schnapps into a blender along with some ice cream, a little White Crème de Cacao and a dash of cinnamon, and you have a concoction that tastes like apple pie with ice cream.

Then came a multitude of fruit flavored schnapps. Many of them are very tasty. Butterscotch flavored schnapps, called Butterschotts, is especially good when mixed with Bailey's. Some moron named this drink a "Slippery Nipp...," Forget it, I can't even finish the name. Seriously, have you ever tried Butterschotts?!?! I swear to God you could pour it over pancakes!!!!

Now, if you are a novice drinker, beware of the wonderful world of Schnapps. As close as it is to being a kid in a candy store, it will sneak up in you. See, you could choke down some of the aforementioned rot gut, get a buzz, and then puke. Or, you could drink this stuff that tastes harmless, get a buzz, and then puke. It's still alcohol, or the liquid version of a "wolf in sheep's clothing."

OUZO

It tastes like black licorice. I don't like black licorice, but we drank it anyways. Why, you ask? Because it DIDN'T taste like gin, vodka, rum, whiskey, Scotch, Bourbon or tequila. Oh yeah, and it was fun to watch it turn cloudy when ice was added. No one wanted to drink it that way, it sucked. When was the last time you wanted "chilled licorice?" It's a good sign you don't need any more if you're dropping in ice to watch it turn cloudy. You know it's time to go home when this becomes a group activity.

BEER

Even though this is the beer category, I'm going to start with a couple of whines.

Number one: "What kind of beer do you have?" Most of the time this would be a normal question, but more often than not, it is asked in a whiney, nasally tone that makes nails on a chalk board sound like music. Whenever you hear that, you KNOW that they will not like any of the beers that you have on hand. You could ramble off thirty different beers and they will still ask, "Do you have (fill in the blank)?"

"Did I say that? If you had been listening, you would know that we don't carry that brand!"

"Why not?"

"Just to make your life miserable. Would you like one or the brands we DO carry, or would you like to let the rest of the people at the table order, before we close?"

"But it's only seven o'clock."

"Quick! Get me some ear plugs or a stun gun! There's that whiney tone again. Maybe the rest of you folks would like to sit at a different table."

Famous whine number two: "I only drink imported beer."

I always want to pose a hypothetical question to these supposed connoisseurs of things foreign, "If you were at a picnic, it's 90 degrees outside, you're sitting in the shade losing weight from an over abundance of perspiration, no air conditioning in sight, and the only beer is Budweiser, sitting in a tub of ice, every bottle completely submerged, and you know that first swallow is gonna be ice, ice cold, are you going to stand on ceremony and say, "I only drink imported beer? I DON'T FREAKING THINK SO!!!"

Okay, back to the beer.....

I know, I shouldn't be so hard on the beer drinkers. For the most part they are pretty easy to get along with. Usually they ask one of two questions, "What have you got on tap?" or "What have you got in a bottle?" Sometimes they ask both.

A typical informational exchange with a beer drinker would go as follows:

"What kind of beer do you have in bottles?"

"We have Miller, Miller Lite, Bud, Bud Lite, Michelob, Michelob Lite, Heineken, Corona, Red Dog and Leinenkugel's."

"Oh, okay, what have you got on tap."

"We have Miller Lite and Labatt Blue."

"Oh, okay, have you got Labatt Blue in a Bottle?"

"No, that would be on tap."

"Oh, okay, did you say you had Corona Lite in a bottle?"

"No, just regular Corona."

"Oh, okay, do you have…"

"Here, I'll just open the cooler doors, and when you see what you want, you just let me know."

"Oh, okay."

And you thought I was being mean asking his friends if they wanted to sit someplace else.

WINE

Wine has gotten a lot more popular over the last fifteen or twenty years. However, if you are thinking of being a wine snob, your time is wasted on me. Like some of the liquors we talked about earlier, I never acquired a taste for wine, either, until I found the one that went well with chocolate. I think dry wine tastes like liquid dust. I don't go around licking dusty furniture, and I don't drink dry wine.Wines that are supposed to be fruity, well, that's lost on me too. Did they mix the fruit with window cleaner so it could achieve that face-making flavor? It wouldn't hurt my feelings if they just used grapes for making jam.

One evening one of the waitri was approaching the service bar, and said one her customers wanted to know what the brand name was of the house Chablis. I told her it was "Bob's." She looked (to her credit), a little puzzled, but one of the ladies at the bar immediately chimed in with, "Oh, I've had it before. It's really good." So, she went on her merry way and reported back to her customer that the house brand was "Bob's." The customer looked a wee bit puzzled also, but she was obviously a good sport, as she agreed to try it.

I know what you're thinking. "BOB's?" How could anyone fall for that? But if you count the waitress and the customer, we're two for two. That's pretty good in anybody's book.

Sometimes you just got to let it go, and appreciate the humor and creativity all found in an evening's conversation.

One of the wines that increased in popularity was Chardonnay. On any given Friday, I would have two or three Chardonnay drinkers at the bar. In order to keep the wine chilled, and easily at hand, I would place it in the beer mug cooler. On any given Friday evening, the Chardonnay drinkers could very well find themselves drinking a Chardonnay Slush, due to my over-chilling of the wine. If they complain, I give them three choices. I can take their glass of slushy wine back into the kitchen and microwave it, they can hold the glass between their legs, or they can take the high road, and this by far is the wisest choice, they can just shut up.

PEOPLE WHO ARE VERY IMPRESSED WITH THEMSELVES

These people are really easy to spot. In fact you don't even have to lay eyes on them. They are the ones who are very impressed with their own drink ordering abilities and the ability to differentiate between a good drink and bad drink. Or so they think. Remember, "think" is the operative word here.

So, some clown at a table, who's very impressed with himself, orders a very, very, very dry as the Sahara Desert martini.

First, let's talk about martinis. A martini is made with gin and dry vermouth, a nasty wine type product. A vodka martini is made with vodka and that same nasty vermouth. We'll talk about all those other martinis (the ones that recently popped up at "martini bars") later.

The trend for the 25 years I tended bar, was that people wanted their martinis dryer and dryer. A dry martini is one that is made with less vermouth, although there never was much vermouth in a martini to begin with. They would request that you just put a drop of vermouth in, or just wave the bottle over the glass. In other words, what they really wanted, but were too chicken to order, was a glass of gin, or vodka. But that just doesn't sound as impressive as a martini. Somewhere along the line, I think it was when James Bond hit the scene, a martini became very cool. Especially when one ordered a "dry martini." Ordering a glass of gin on the rocks just doesn't sound cool or sophisticated. It makes you sound like a lush. But a rose by any other name…. As time went on, I discovered that no one really wanted any vermouth, (I told you it was nasty), but they would still order a "dry,dry,dry,dry, I cannot impress upon you enough how dry I want this" martini.

So, instead of getting drinks returned, I hit upon a solution! I quit putting vermouth in the martinis! For years, I never even picked up a vermouth bottle. People would compliment me, and said I made a "mean martini." One guy stated, "I wish you could teach my wife to make a martini like this." I would just smile and nod and say, "Thank you." I kept my smirk to myself.

Now that we have some background, let's get back to Mr. Dry-dry-dry-as-the-Sahara Desert martini clown. This is not an isolated incident, by the way. You pour the martini, completely omitting the vermouth, so what they have is straight gin or vodka, poured over ice, with an olive or a lemon twist, if that is their preference. The waitress delivers the drinks to the table and a few minutes later is back with the Sahara Desert martini. Mr. Clown loudly announced to the table that there was WAY TOO MUCH VERMOUTH in his martini. So, she brings it back, and I ask her if Mr. Clown can see me. She says, "No, they are sitting in the front room." So this means he can't see me at all. The reason I ask is that I don't want him to be able to watch me pour the same drink into another glass and send it back.

A short time later I asked the waitress how Mr. Clown's "second martini" was. She told me he said it was perfect. Asshole. So what did we learn from this? That the idiot Mr. Clown really doesn't know what he is talking about, but he is sure impressed with himself.

Now, let's get back to those stupid wannbe martinis that are popping up at "martini bars."

Like I said earlier, a martini is made with gin, vodka, and supposedly vermouth. If you want to get trashed, drink a few martinis. This would work best if you have no taste buds. Let's face it (and we all know my feelings about gin), it should be used to clean paint brushes. In all the years I tended bar, I found absolutely no redeeming qualities in gin. It stinks, it tastes worse than it smells, and it gives everything you mix it with a foul taste. Vodka may be slightly more palatable. It isn't as distasteful when mixed with other things, like shoe polish. BUT!!! Whoever said vodka had no taste, was either a liar, a full blown alcoholic. Or again, he had no taste buds.

So now you're wondering, "Why would anyone want to drink a martini?" There are two reasons, the first is because there is such a "coolness" about ordering a martini, and the second is you want to drink straight alcohol. Since there is such a "coolness" associated with the word martini, it's just a natural that a "martini bar" would draw a big crowd. So they started making up drinks and put the word martini in the name so everyone would think that they too were now "cool" because they were drinking a martini.

Let's backtrack yet again. What did I tell you was in a martini? It's gin or vodka and supposedly vermouth. So, if that's what a martini is, then how can some drink that contains none of those ingredients be a martini?

Ordering a chocolate martini is equivalent to ordering a prime rib made out of salmon. Quite frankly, the thought of mixing chocolate with gin makes my stomach hurt. Even the chocolate is cringing. Oh, but wait! There isn't any gin in a chocolate martini! It's made out of all those sissy liquors most men don't even want to mention, even when they are ordering for their wife. These would all be considered "ladies" drinks, and no real man would be caught dead drinking them.

Most of the new martini drinks are drinks that no one would order if they had a different name. What if a raspberry martini was called a Raspberry Fruit Boy? Would anyone outside of Los Angeles order it?

But I've got to hand it to the marketing directors on this one, they sure found a way to get frou-frou or wussy drinks to become acceptable. This brings us to Strawberry Daiquiris. Strawberry Daiquiris are a great, refreshing, "I don't like the taste of alcohol" drink. They are made with strawberries (that was a real no brainer), rum and sour mix. Most bars use a commercially made sour mix, which is very good. You would be hard pressed to reproduce the flavor on your own, so why bother? Next, you throw these ingredients into the bar blender, along with some ice, and blend away. The ice makes it nice and cold and thick. A good bar blender can crush ice in no time at all. In fact, these blenders are so powerful that they can puree your entire steak dinner to the consistency of baby food in thirty seconds. Usually we had two blender units, but only one was ever working at a time. But, on the plus side, we had about four blender cups, or containers, so you could keep one for strawberry drinks, one for plain old sours, and one for those don't-ever-order-them-on-my-shift fucking ice cream drinks. Oh yeah, the fourth one. That one we try not to use. It cuts down on the clean up.

Another refreshing strawberry drink is the Strawberry Margarita. Okay here we go, it's made with...that's right, straaaaaawberries (took you long enough) and a Margarita mix we make up ahead of time because we go through quite a bit of it. It is made of tequila, triple sec, and (da-da) a margarita mix. Some may think this is cheating, well, so what. You'll never know it anyways, and it tastes great. Now, the process is the same as a Strawberry Daiquiri. You throw all this crap in a blender, add ice, and you have instant, frozen Strawberry Margarita, which, in reality, tastes A WHOLE LOT like a Strawberry Daiquiri. I've seen many a person who cannot tell the difference.

I know, you're wondering where all this is leading to, well, it brings us to the group of "buttheads." We all know some of these. They order a drink but want to change all the ingredients.

IT'S TOO LATE ON A FRIDAY TO START MIXING THIS SHIT

Every now and then, we would get a late night group from one of the nearby auto plants (Remember, we are in a suburb of Detroit, where it's mandatory that everyone be within walking distance of an auto plant.), who like to come in and order drinks that would gag a maggot and have all connoisseurs of fine cognac, past and present, rolling over in their graves.

Knowing that the ordering process for this group was going to be more painful than getting a root canal, without any drugs, the waitress draaaaaaged herself over to the table once again. Meanwhile, those sitting at the bar and myself rudely snicker about the ordeal she is about to go through. Oh well, tough shit, better her than me.

When having an order taken at a table, most people wait their turn to order, but not this group. They like to start their order before the previous one has stopped speaking. Now, you're wondering what's so hard about ordering a few drinks. Nothing! Unless you happen to be a complete and total butthead, like most of this group. Most tables would go in turn, such as, "I'll have a frozen Margarita, please," and, "I'd like a bottle of Bud Lite."

"May I have a Bacardi and Coke, with lime, please, and she'll have a Bailey's on the rocks."

Simple, right? Now let me show you how this group works.

"Okay, I want a Strawberry Margarita, but leave out the tequila and put in Courvoisier and rim the glass--"

"I want the same thing but without the Courvoisier, use Hennessey instead and put in extra tequila--"

"--berry Daiquiri, but not frozen, I want some chunks of--"

"Make my Margarita with Chivas Regal and Hennessey, no salt on the--"

"--extra lime. I want five large pieces of fresh li—"

"I want Courvoisier and Coke--"

"Remember I don't want tequila in my Stra..."

"--Heineken."

"--sugar on the rim of the one with..."

"--if there's too much strawberry, I'm gonna send it back."

When the waitress makes the journey back over the River Styx to the service bar, we sort out the order as best we can. I get out my "strawberry blender cup" and commence mixing these abominations of alcohol and fruit. Hennessey and Courvoisier are cognacs that should NEVER EVER be mixed with ANYTHING! They are a sipping drink that should be enjoyed straight up or on the rocks, but never, ever mixed. (Don't make me say it again.)

Both the waitress and I only have a vague idea of what these drinks should be. Part of that is because the ordering process was so convoluted, and partly because it's late, and we don't care. So, I told her as long as we get them in the correct glasses, we'll be fine. The Strawberry Daiquiri glass is a long-stemmed "Tulip glass" and the Margarita glass looks like a bowl on a stem.

Off she goes with all these concoctions (that really should be illegal) to set them down and see how many are going to be sent back, with some idiotic complaint.

All is quiet for a moment. Then the complaining begins. One of the strawberry drinks doesn't have enough Courvoisier in it (she can't taste it), and another has too much sour mix. Only two come back on the first round. I do my usual "Can they see me?" Instead of re-making these glasses of frozen swill, I drizzle a few drops of Courvoisier on top of both of them, and get a little on the rim. They'll taste it now.

Five minutes later, another drink comes back. It's half gone. The complaint is that it was too frozen. I'm always amused when something gets sent back that is half gone.

"You mean it took you that long to figure out it was too frozen? What's wrong with you? Have you got permanent brain freeze?" They are usually trying to get another WHOLE drink, with out having to pay for it. DOESN'T WORK!

I drizzled a little cheap tequila in it and stir it around. When I'm in a really good mood, I light the tequila with a match first, but just as a precautionary measure to insure that the drink is no longer too frozen. Dumb fucks.

The four regulars who are sitting at the bar are really getting a kick out of this now. They know how much I hate to dirty up the blender when it's late and had already been cleaned once.

As the waitress sets up the glasses for the next round: some salt, no salt, half salt. I start pouring stuff into the blender. This time I start out with a mess of strawberries (these are canned strawberries, by the way), then I add some Courvoisier, and then some Hennessey, and then some tequila, and then some sour mix, and then some Margarita mix. Mark, who's sitting at the bar, looks at me with a puzzled look on his face and asks me what I'm doing. Why am I pouring all that stuff in the blender? I told him I was tired of mixing all these garbage drinks separately. When you mix all that stuff with strawberries, it all starts to taste the same after a while, so I was saving time by mixing it all at once.

I put the blender cup on the base, gave it a one second whirl, pulled it off, and poured the mostly unblended, ungodly mess into one of the margarita glasses. Then I threw some ice into the blender, and whirled the rest into a frozen mess. I poured it into the remaining margarita and daiquiri glasses, and sent it off to the table. No drinks were sent back that time.

The guys at the bar were highly amused, and massively awed. Dumb fucks.

MORE ORDERING "DON'TS"

DO NOT swagger up to the bar and order "Two fingers" of whiskey. That is old, out-dated, and probably only happened in the movies. Those who made the silly decision to order this way found out that they got pretty much what they ordered. I would hold the glass between my thumb and first two fingers, with my fingers INSIDE the glass, and then proceed to pour the alcohol of their choice down my fingers and into the glass. Is that not what they ordered? As said, buffoon stood there with chin hitting the floor, I would smile sweetly and tell them, "Don't worry. The alcohol kills all the germs." I then set down the glass and go along my merry way to whatever needs to be done next.

DO NOT order ANYTHING in a style you think will be like James Bond. James Bond is not a REAL person, so get out of your fantasy world of thinking you could be like him. Even if he were real, you couldn't be that cool in three life times, let alone the time it takes to order a drink.

One of the regulars decided to try and order like James Bond. He asked for his martini to be shaken, not stirred. So...I picked up the large glass we use to mix a martini when it is to be served "up." (That means chilled, stirred, and then strained into a little martini glass.) I put some ice into the mixing glass; I poured in the gin, passed my hand over the vermouth bottle without picking it up, and shook the mixing glass. You know, when you shake something that has no lid on it, there are times when some of the contents have a way of displacing themselves over the edge of the glass. Who knew? When I was through "shaking" and "not stirring," there was about a half a martini left. I poured it into the martini glass and set it down in front of the poor, misguided James Bond wannabe.

He looked at his half-a-drink, and then looked up at me, and then looked back at his drink, and then looked back at me. He looked perplexed. Just as he started to open his mouth to utter what would surely be more foolishness, I told him, "Perhaps it would have been better to leave the method of mixing up to the professional." The rest of the crowd nodded silently in agreement.

"Huh?"

DO NOT SAY "GIMME"

Picture this, you're a kid sitting at the diner table, and you look over at your mother and say, "Gimme the mashed potatoes." In many circumstances, this would be met with a reprimand or a smack upside the head while being berated for having poor table manors. Then your father would get in on the act, hit you in the arm, and tell you "Don't talk to your mother that way!" Where's your manners! You ASK for things, you don't demand them!"

WHACK!!! (That was either parent hitting you upside the head, again, just to drive the point home).

"You may have the mashed potatoes when you learn to ask for them in a civil manner."

It's important to remember the lessons you learned as a kid. If you sit down at the bar and say "Gimme a beer," no one is going to run and get Your Highness a beer like they were in training for the bartender decathlon. A more likely scenario is that you will quickly be brought back to reality when you feel the menu make contact with the side of your head, and you mother's voice is echoing in your ears. "Where's your manners! Were you raised in a barn?!?"

If you are one of those exceedingly foolish individuals who would prefer to wear their beer, as opposed to drinking it, keep up with the "Gimme." You'll soon see the contents of a beer mug come splashing in your direction. If you choose to duck to avoid being splashed, just make sure none of the splashing beer puts out Helen's cigarette. Should that happen, the repercussions are too ugly to mention. Suffice it to say the aftermath of that will make me look like sweet little Shirley Temple.

CALLING IN YOUR ORDER
(No, this is not about carry outs)

The Saturday day shift usually started out pretty slow, so it became the "house cleaning shift." All the bottles were wiped down, all the little shelves the bottles sat on were cleaned, as well as the shelves under the end of the bar that held condiments, back up liquor bottles, and anything else we felt needed to be put there, you know, like, extra cigarettes, nail polish, Nicorette and a Rubik's Cube. If it was really slow then you just kept wiping and polishing every surface area whether it needed it or not.

On one of these extremely slow starting Saturdays, I was fortunate enough to have been chosen for the day shift. There was one guy at the bar. Just one. He was in his own little world of television, having it all to himself, and I was in my own little world of cleaning. I became a woman obsessed with making sure everything was going to be shiny, like new. As I was deeply engrossed in the different color light patterns that come off of the pretty colored liquids in the bottles (I was playing with a flashlight), and the one patron at the bar was engrossed in the television (or so I thought), the hostess informed me that I had a phone call. I walked to the end of the bar, picked up the phone, said "Hello?" I couldn't figure who would be calling me.

"Hi Gretchen, this is Ben, you know, the only guy sitting at the bar. Could I have another drink, please?"

I had gotten so involved in my cleaning, I forgot all about the one customer who was sitting there. I felt so, so...interrupted.

Mind you, we didn't have cell phones yet, so he had to get up and go into the phone booth. Since I couldn't see who was in the phone booth from behind the bar, I thought he went to use the restroom. Whoops.

OH, THE
SILLY THINGS WE BET ON.....

Ed and Loretta have been coming in on Saturday evening for quite a while now. They're both in their fifties, approaching retirement, been together thirty l-o-n-g years. One thing I've noticed about couples who have been together a l-o-n-g time is, the longer they've been together, the more they talk to other people. When they do communicate, it's usually something like this:

Loretta elbows Ed and says, "Isn't that right, Ed?," and Ed replies "Uh-huh," without ever taking his eyes off of "Wheel of Fortune." (Ed is one of Vanna's biggest fans.) You'd think after thirty l-o-n-g years Ed would be tired of being elbowed and jabbed, but he just "Uh-huhs" much the same way one would absent-mindedly swat at a fly. Every now and then, we hear him utter a letter, such as "K," as he lets us know what his choice for the "Wheel" puzzle would have been.

In order for all the patrons to keep track of who's who, most are known for something other than their names. It might be for where you like to sit, such as the couple who always sits at the curve of the bar (It's the best place to watch the cooks), or the guy who looks like C. Everett Koop, the former Surgeon General, or the woman with the unusual hair color because nature didn't give that color to ANYONE. (I believe you met her earlier) Ed and Loretta are known as "That guy" and "his wife with the tremendously huge tits." We're talking REALLY big here! They're like a giant mammaric shelf. (No, you won't find that word in the dictionary, but sometimes it's necessary to form a word to get your point across in a more exact manner. Oh, and HA! HA! I thought of it and you didn't!). Actually, I cut the description short so you would get an accurate idea of the amplitude of this mammaric shelf. The full description is "That guy and his wife with the tremendously huge tits who NEVER fails to drop food on them."

Hence, one of the silly things we bet on.

The bet here is not whether Loretta will or will not drop food on herself, but rather how long will that food will remain on the down slope of those Grand Teton twin peaks. In order to pull off the bet discreetly, your bar crowd must consist of a lot of regular customers. In fact, we're so cool, those not in the know have no idea anything is even going on. The first priority is to find out what Loretta is having for dinner that evening, which is not hard to do, since everyone at the bar discusses the menu, what's on special for the night, what they've had before, can you put up wallpaper with the split pea soup, do the salmon patties have real salmon in them, etc. In reality, the food is actually very good, or these people would not keep coming back week after week for ten or fifteen years. It also promotes discussion when one asks for a menu, and I tell them "NO! Share with the guy next to you! Waddya think?!?! We've got one menu for everybody in here? You people have got to learn how to share. Besides that, Bob needs help with the big words." See, now it's not just sharing, it's community service for the multi-syllabically impaired.

We can usually count on Loretta herself to start the discussion on what she's going to have this evening since she has to find out what Ed is having so she won't order the same item. After all, she's going to be sampling his dinner also, so that can complicate things. If Ed has spaghetti and meatballs, there's a good chance she could try to get too much on her fork while sampling and lose part of it en route to her mouth. Or, if she ordered a French dip and dripped the au jus on herself, that'll just soak in and stay there for the rest of the evening.

All bettors are allowed to place their bets in thirty second time segments, starting from the time the food first lands on said mammaric shelf, until the time it rolls off back onto the plate. Another thing a bettor has to take into consideration is some of the basic laws of physics. (This is not just a night out at the bar; it's an education.) Obviously a solid object, such as a green bean, will have a faster fall time than a partially solid food substance such as mashed potatoes, where one has to consider the ability of the mashed potatoes to cling to the fabric before making a downward descent, and how much will "drag" affect said descent of mashed potatoes, and how much will the type of fabric upon which said mashed potatoes land affect the drag time? Whew!

This is not for amateurs.

Ed has ordered a French dip and a cup of chicken noodle soup, some dork on "Wheel of Fortune" just wasted his money on two vowels, and Loretta decided on the lasagna. Remember, this will be preceded by a salad, which she will assemble herself at the salad bar, putting a serious dent in the ranch dressing.

As Loretta ambles her way to the salad bar, and the rest of the crowd parts like the Red Sea so as not to get knocked into an adjacent booth should she turn too fast, the bettors place their bets. This is done very discreetly. Remember, these people have a lot of practice at bar-betting subterfuge. It's a first come, first serve situation. The first one to write their time on bar stationary (bevnaps) and subtly place it on a spot where I can pick it up, obviously, gets first pick. All these people have considered all the options and variables that can happen with lasagna, and that Loretta is wearing a sweater. Couples usually bet as one and have a discussion between them. Dave and Betty have placed their bet first. As I go over and get their betting slip, I look and see what time they've chosen, to make sure no else selects the same time slot. They have chosen thirty seconds to one minute. We can see from their choice, they're playing middle of the road and hoping the lasagna will stay for at lest thirty seconds, but not more than one minute. I think they're counting on the fibers of the sweater to create a small amount of drag.

Another slip comes, it's Bob and Shirley, and they've

chosen zero to thirty seconds. They're hoping for Loretta to be so zealous about her eating that she is bending over her plate, scarfing down the food, and thus creating a steeper angle of descent. I TOLD you this wasn't for amateurs. OH! As I look out of the corner of my eye, I see another betting slip placed on the bar. It's Vern. I walk over and chat for a minute, pick up the bevnap, unfold it, and Vern has neatly written, "I just sneezed on this. Thanks for throwing it out." We'll get back at Vern later.

Just as the betting is about to come to a close, I see an almost imperceptible nod from Jerry and Julie. He and his wife have gone with "longer than anyone else's time."

That was easy. There were no duplicate times chosen, everyone anted up (I have the money in my pocket), and now we just have to await the results.

Let the eating begin!

Da da daaa da da da daa daaaa... (Jeopardy! Music) da da daa da... and the first few forkfuls make a clean sweep into the masticating chamber.

Do I see a piece of lettuce sliding off of the fork?!? Ohhhhh, she got it!!!

Here goes another, and WHAM!!!! The lettuce has landed!

(We didn't even make it to the lasagna.) The clock starts. The dressing (ranch) is holding it in place. Oh wait a minute... I think I see a little slippage.... Okay, it appears to have stabilized...still sitting there.... Loretta is sniffing...she's raising her head...higher...higher...higher.... Then her entire body heaves back and she lets loose with a tremendous sneeze!!! Whoa! Didn't see that one coming!! The lettuce didn't stand a chance. Let's see, we're at two minutes and ten seconds. Jerry and Julie have won. Vern is now trying to claim the prize, saying he should win by default, since he sneezed into his betting sheet aka bevnap. No one is buying it.

THE COUPLE THAT PLAYS TOGETHER....

Every now and then you run into a couple whose motto is "The couple that plays together, stays together." But, have you ever run into a couple whose motto is "The couple that quaffs down mass quantities of alcohol together stays together"? No? I didn't think so. If you do, run very fast. Don't ever engage them in a conversation. You'll regret it and find yourself looking over your shoulder for the rest of your life.

Meet Cal and Anita. On the surface, they seem like a good natured, fun-loving couple. But after about one minute (or less) of conversation, you realize they are plastered. And they stay that way most of the time. I think their blood is eighty proof. They are functioning on borrowed brain cells. After five minutes with them, you start to wish that the part of the brain that controls their speech would just shut down.

I made a HUGE mistake one evening when Cal and Anita were sitting at the bar waiting for a table. I was chatting with them for a few minutes, and then I got lucky and they were called for their table. As they were leaving, I said, "Enjoy your dinner. Stop by later. We'll chat." I say that to a lot of people, but most knew it was just idle chatter. But I learned later that night that Cal and Anita took it literally.

The place is nearly empty, it's getting late, and here they come, drinks in hand, sloshing out of the glass, making a bee-line for the bar. "Well, you said to come back and chat, so here we are!" It's amazing that they still had control of most of their motor skills. My immediate reaction was to utter a bunch of expletives to myself. (What the hell!! Oh fuck!!!) I couldn't believe they took me seriously! What really poured salt on the wound was that they were soon to be the last ones there, and if they would just leave, then I could, too.

The fates were not with me that night. As soon as they sat down, they both started chirping away. At the same time. Neither one took any breaths when they spoke. The only thing I understood was when either of them said, "To make a long story short...," and they said that a lot! I just kept looking from one to the other and back again, and again, because there was obviously no need for me to speak; they had that totally covered. Not that I could get a word in edgewise, even if I did care to try.

It was amazing in its own way. They kept telling me stories at the same time. It seemed that neither was aware that the other one was speaking, or that I wasn't really listening to either of them. I have no idea what they were babbling on about. To look at them you would have thought they were addressing a group of thirty who were all totally enraptured with their tales. After a while,

I wasn't sure if they were still speaking English. One could get just as much out of their ramblings if the two of them were sitting behind a glass wall in a soundproof room. They gestured, they laughed, and they laughed so hard they slapped their thighs. It wouldn't have surprised me a bit if Rod Serling had suddenly appeared and told me I had just entered "The Twilight Zone."

You try not to look at the clock when stuck in these circumstances because you could swear the hands just moved backwards. Pretty soon, you don't even hear them anymore. You just start fantasizing what you would do if you had a gun, with only one bullet. As you start to contemplate the options, your face begins to take on different expressions. (Which they always misinterpret as interest in their stories.) First, you think maybe you could shoot Cal, but he wouldn't feel it. He could watch you as you hit him over the head with a shovel and not know anything happened. As you smile to yourself (another misinterpretation on their part), you picture him slowly falling off of the bar stool, still talking, hitting the floor, and Anita saying, "For God's sake, Cal. Get up! You've still gotta drive home."

Or, you could shoot Anita. Again, you get a little grin on your face as you picture her falling on the floor, still chattering away, and Cal saying, "Won't be the first time I had to drag her out to the car."

OR...you could shoot yourself in the foot and tell them you have to seek emergency medical treatment. Their solution, "Just pour some vodka on it, honey. It'll be fine in the morning."

And then!!! You realize you just daydreamed your way to closing time!!! Of course, being seasoned, professional drinkers, they don't miss a beat and ask what happened to last call? Quick! Now I have to punt! I tell them we already had it twenty minutes ago, and I grab two empty glasses from the sink and say "See! Here's your old ones!" smiling all the while.

Okay, that was a little lame, but it worked, and that's all that mattered.

Next time they came in, I ducked into the kitchen when I saw them coming. Don't cluck your tongue at me. You'd do the same thing!

MORE REGULARS

We used to get a lot of couples whose kids were grown and gone, or mostly so. They would come in for dinner two or three times a week. Many of these women had cooked for families for years and were now semi-retired from the kitchen. I made a lot of good friends talking to these people. After all, when you see these people a few times a week, that's more times than you see your relatives.

One such couple was Burt and Joann. After getting to know them, Joann and I discovered that we were in the same bowling league about fifteen years earlier. Her team was in first place, and mine was in last. So, uh-huh, we had that in common. Burt and Joann were people that you looked forward to seeing. You knew you could just have a normal conversation. They were also my dog's grandparents. When I was moving into my house, I promised my then two year old son, that he could have a dog. I mentioned this to Joann, and she told to wait until summer. One of her daughter's dogs was pregnant. So I did, and we ended up with an adorable, mostly Black Labrador, female puppy, that my son promptly named "Spike."

Needless to say, Joann was disappointed in her grand puppy's name, but she knew I had promised my son he could name the puppy and couldn't go back on my word. Joann decided to refer to the puppy as "Spikette." I thought that was worse, but few argued with Joann. (I liked Joann's attitude and sort of thought of her as a mentor.) If anyone tried, her husband would just smile and wish the "arguer" good luck.

Joann was one of the few people in this world who really knew just how empty a beer keg was. If she tasted her beer and said it was near the bottom, two or three pulls later, it would run out. The woman had a gift. Being a regular at the bar, she also knew that when she told me the beer was almost out or pointed out that there were no bubbles in her glass, that there may be some repercussions.

One night when it was pretty crowded, she called down to me at the end of the bar to tell me there was no fizz in her beer and to point out there were no bubbles floating in the glass. I walked down to the service end of the bar, grabbed two long straws, walked back over to Joann, put the straws in her glass and started blowing into them. After creating sufficient foam, I said,

"There are your bubbles! Are you happy now?!"

What the hell, I was going to give here a new beer anyways. A new beer from the new keg.

IT'S ALL IN THE NAME

If you think having two Patty's at the bar is confusing, well, it's actually not. We ALWAYS call one Patty "Patty Duke" because she looks just like her, and the other is just Patty, except when it's just us workers talking among ourselves, when she is called "Painful Patty," which is a more polite version of "Pain-in-the-ass Patty."

So now, enter into the equation some more Pattys. And you thought this was going to be easy. We had a bartender/waitress that we called Patricia-Patty, and another bartender/waitress that we called Patty-Patty. Those of us that worked there were able to keep it straight, it was the customers that had problems, and not just with names.

For example: A conversation with the boss's son, "I was talking to Patricia-Patty the other day, and she told me that Patty-Patty asked her to cover her Saturday bar shift, but how about if I cover Patty-Patty's bar shift and Patricia-Patty just works the floor, that way she can get out early since she is also working the day shift?"

He ponders that for a quick moment, "Yeah, that'll work. OH! And Painful Patty has been her usual 'Never understood the concept of subtlety-self' and telling everyone that will listen, that

Saturday is one of the anniversaries of her twenty-first birthday, so don't forget to defrost a birthday cake."

"Oh, I won't forget," I quickly reassure him.

These birthday cakes are cute little round cakes, about six inches across that we get from a local baker. They come to us so frozen that a hammer wouldn't make a dent in it when first taken out of the freezer. Since it IS Painful Patty, the question now is, do I give her a slightly frozen cake, and watch her try and saw through it with a butter knife, OR...Do I put it under the heat lamps to thaw it quickly, only to bring it back with half-melted frosting, and that "Leaning Tower of Pisa" look?

Now, let's have the same conversation with one of the customers.

"I'm going to be working Patty-Patty's Saturday night shift."

Helen asks, "Is that the Patty with the long hair?"

I explain, "They both have long hair. Patty-Patty is the one who also DOES hair. Patricia -Patty is the one with the glasses."

Helen again, "So, then you're working with Patricia-Patty, and Patty -Patty is working the floor?"

"No, I'm working by myself, Patricia-Patty is working the floor, and Patty-Patty won't be here at all, but Painful Patty (Helen is one of the few customers privy to that nickname), will be here because it's her birthday, and Patty Duke will be here because it's Saturday, so you see, either Patty-Patty or Patricia-Patty had to take the night off in order to adhere to our 'Three-Patty-a-night' rule."

Helen then responds, "Explain this again later after I've had a few drinks. It might make more sense then."

THEN...We had three Nancy's at one time. We were always trying to find ways to differentiate between the three of them. "Always," being the operative word here. We started calling one "Young Nancy," which naturally segued into calling another, "Old Nancy," but she did not care for that name.

"Now everyone will know that I'm the oldest."

"No, they won't. We'll them it's because you were here the longest."

Then the third Nancy enters the conversation, "So I get to be just plain Nancy?"

"Well, 'Just Plain Nancy,' is a lot to spit out," I point out to her.

"No," she moans back, "Not 'Just Plain Nancy,' just Nancy."

So I tell her, "You're gonna have to make your mind. Do you want to be called Just Nancy, or Just Plain Nancy?"

"Neither," she answers in an exasperated tone. "Just...Nancy."

"Okay, I've got this figured out now. We have Young Nancy, Old Nancy, and Just Nancy."

"NNOOOOOO," two of the three Nancy's wail.

Young Nancy is not complaining, Old Nancy now declares she wants to be "Best Nancy," Just Nancy is till trying to figure out the last conversation, and then Young Nancy now decides she wants to be "Pretty Nancy."

Then someone pipes in with, "How about Nancy One, Nancy Two, and Nancy Three?"

"How BOOORRRRRRRIIIINNNNNNG!"

Besides, then they'll argue about whether the designation of Nancy One is interpreted as the oldest, first, or best. We could go with Short Nancy, Tall Nancy and Big Nancy, but they'll find something derogatory in that, too.

You know, "Hey you" works for me.

Other people get nicknames, but not because there is a gaggle of Marys or Karens. It just seems to happen naturally, just as the tides ebb and flow. Mary was eighteen when she started working with us. She still had braces on her teeth. It was the first summer we were open. She was a little shy at first, but got over it VERY quickly!

We used to have a large group from one of the nearby auto plants, (different from the last group) that came in when the afternoon shift was done. They used to arrive en masse, with tires squealing as they approached the parking lot. Since they had a limited amount of time to drink, closing time was a real challenge. We had to have everyone out by 2:30 a.m.

The first time I told Mary to go pick up ALL the glasses, whether they were empty or not, she replied, "I can't take a glass if they haven't finished yet."

I told her in no uncertain terms, "Yes, you can!!! It's your job. It's the law!"

"OOOHHHHH……."

Within a week, she was grabbing glasses, cans, and bottles off the tables like she was a Viking Queen.

She had a bunch of glasses on her tray one night, and one guy was following behind with his mouth still on the straw, to get those last few sips out of the drink. She never slowed down. He almost had to run to keep up with her.

Within a couple of weeks, everyone realized that you just didn't mess with Mary. She was a lot of fun, but she had a way of giving you that "Stern Nun" look at closing time, and the guys knew she meant business. Thus, she became known as "Sister Mary Braces."

Our next "Mary" nickname may not be considered as flattering as "Sister Mary Braces," but it was taken good-naturedly, with a splash of fun. As if there was a choice.

"Why is everyone calling that girl Moo?" Mach wanted to know.

"Oh, it's short for Moo Cow," Helen explained.

"Moo Cow! But the girl is skinny as a rail!"

"Yes, but her name is Mary Catherine."

"What's that got to do with anything?"

"He doesn't get it, does he, Helen?" asked the Bar Wench.

"No more than he understands why we call him Mach. Why don't you give it a try?"

"Hey, Mach let one side of your brain rest for a while. We can see the smoke. The reason we call her Moo is Mary Catherine was a lot to say, so we shortened it to M.C. Then, cleverly realizing one day that M.C. could also stand for "Moo Cow," we started calling her that." (It was, too, clever!) It wasn't long before the customers started to catch on and began to call her Moo Cow. As names have a way of becoming abbreviated, she was soon known simply as "Moo." It wasn't unusual to hear someone request, "May we have Moo's section, please?"

You've heard of "Zena, Warrior Princess," or whatever she was called, or "Sheena, Queen of the Jungle?" We have "Helen, Ultimate Queen Bitch of the Universe," AKA Mt. St. Helen. Up to this point, you thought she was just this nice bar fly, trying to make life easy for the foreign guy from Massachusetts.

This wasn't a title those of us at the bar gave her. She earned this at work at GM (General Motors). A group of the guys she worked with put it to a vote one night at the bar. They had been tossing this around for a while, and I finally looked at them and said, "Okay, everyone in favor of electing Helen "Ultimate Queen Bitch of the Universe" raise their hand. I thought some of them were going to throw their arms clear out of their shoulder sockets from raising them so quickly. It was a unanimous vote. Some even tried to vote in absentia for those who were not there by raising both hands.

So now we have "Helen, Ultimate Queen Bitch of the Universe," and yours truly, "The Bar Wench from Hell" in the same building. Is it any wonder we get along so well?

As you have already seen, there are many reasons why

some get nicknames. There are times when more than one nickname is merited, such as Helen, AKA Ultimate Queen Bitch of the Universe, AKA Mt. St. Helen, who is also in the running for the "Shortest Female at the Bar" or, to be politically correct, "Most Vertically Challenged." With that many nicknames, you can't help but be popular.

Her main competition for the "Most Vertically Challenged" title was a woman who worked days, (Helen worked afternoons), and was usually at the bar when I arrived at 5:30 p.m. We were talking about height one day, or lack thereof and we decided that Dana was the same height as a full grown Keebler Elf. So, naturally, we started calling her Keebler. How cute. (Grin, damn it!)

Those who were familiar with Keebler and the Queen Bitch said it was a tough call as to who was taller, but getting them to stand next to each other wasn't going to be easy since they were seldom there at the same time. However, we knew, if we were patient, sooner of later it would happen.

There are several factors that need to be considered when determining who is the taller (or shorter) of the two. We have to take into consideration that Helen's hair is generally higher than Keebler's, and we also have to consider the shoes, and whether either of them is cheating, by standing on their toes. (It happens)

As luck would have it, on a Friday night, their shifts just happened to overlap because Helen came in early and Keebler stayed late. The regular Friday night crowd was starting to place their bets.

It was still a tough call, as Helen and Keebler were sitting at opposite ends of the bar. Since neither contestant was eager to win, getting them to cooperate and stand side-by-side wasn't easy.

"I have to go to the restroom."

"I don't feel like getting up right now."

"Maybe in a minute, when I'm feeling taller."

"You can't flatten out the top of my hair."

"I have the wrong shoes on."

"I think the floor slants."

"I'm always taller in the morning."

We finally got them to stand next to each other for about three seconds. Again, too many variables came into play. And, just like a couple of second graders, they couldn't get them to stand still long enough for us to make an educated guess. We looked at shoes and hair, disregarded the lame "slanty floor" excuse, and called it a tie. Besides that, we didn't have any sort of measuring device on hand.

THE BOB CLUB

It was a rule that if you have more than three people with the same name, the you must find a way to differentiate between them, so everyone knows, without a doubt, who you are talking about.

Some names come and go, like Nancy, but you are always

going to have a bunch of Bobs. We have Ol' Bob, Bob Who Spells it Backwards, Bob the Well-Dressed Chef, Bob-O-Link (and avid golfer, not a bird), and several Bob it Doesn't Matter Which Ones, among others.

And, to the fool who chimes in, "Hey, what's my nickname?"

"We never knew your real name. Just be happy we acknowledge you. AND... If you keep bugging us, we'll call you Bob it doesn't Matter Which One."

"But my names not Bob," he whiiiiiiiined.

"Perhaps you weren't paying attention when we said it didn't matter."

THE EDS

Although Ed is not as popular a name as Bob, we have a few examples. We have Brain Dead Ed, Good Looking Ed, Polack Eddie, and Ed the Talking Horse. Good Looking Ed and Polack Eddie are self-explanatory. Let me tell you about the other Eds. Brain Dead Ed was also known as Up-Side-the-Head Ed when we were in a bowling league. Up-Side-the-Head Ed used to wear his hair in a "Fro" so every time someone got a strike, we hit Ed up-side the head. That name died out with the bowling league, and shortly after that he received his new moniker, Brain Dead Ed. For some reason this particular one stuck.

Brain Dead Ed got that handle when he was having a discussion with one of the waitri one night, about nursing, of all things. The waitress he was debating with was a nursing student at the time, and Ed was not. It would appear to the trained observer, or any moron passing by, that they were not in agreement on a certain medical issue. I would definitely give the nursing student the upper hand, having immersed herself in the subject day after day for a few years. But Ed was more stubborn and didn't feel that any classes or training gave ANYONE more knowledge, about anything, when he was certain he was right. Sensing that the discussion was pointless, the waitress/nursing student proclaimed Ed to be brain dead, and hence, the name Brain Dead Ed stuck. You would not believe how quickly it caught on.

Unlike Brain Dead Ed, we did not refer to Ed the Talking Horse as Ed the Talking Horse when he was in the room. It started out as "Mr. Ed," the name given to a certain talking television horse, but anyone younger than us might not know who we were talking about, so we became more descriptive (and we didn't want to insult the real Mr. Ed). Ed became Ed the Talking Horse. It fit. He would sort of bob his head when he was talking and say, "Wweeeelllll nnnooowwwwww," (Whinny it like a horse). Although, if I remember correctly to his credit, he did not snort.

Several people also likened him to the other end of the horse.

OH LOOK! Everyone say Hi! to Pat and Chris, the couple with the interchangeable names! Believe it or not, we actually had two couples named Pat and Chris. I was always grateful that both men were named Chris, and both women (common sense would dictate that this follows) were named Pat. If it had been any different, it would've been back to the nickname drawing board. Do not get these two "Pats" confused with any of the "Pattys" from an earlier discussion. The names are worlds apart. (Just listen, don't ponder).

B.A.

For some, the letters B.A. instantly conjure up the thought "Bachelor of Arts." While this may be true in many instances, it is not true at the bar. It is short for that age old moniker Battle Ax. While engaging in friendly banter one evening, two of our patrons, who work together at GM, got into name calling. He called her an old Battle Ax, and for some reason, it stuck. As time went on (as it is known to do), Battle Ax was shortened to B.A. People were no longer aware of what B.A.'s real name was. When new people would come in, she was introduced as "B.A." She was extremely feisty, and many thought the name fit. I think she secretly liked the name because she tried her hardest to live up to it.

WAITRI, (IT'S THE LATIN PLURAL FOR WAITRESSES)

There are some people in this world that you can always count on. Not all for the same reasons, thank God, that would be awfully boring. But you can always count on Stacy to have a louder and more dramatic reaction than most. That's why we like to tease her. Stacy had a bad habit of dropping things, which wouldn't have been noticed by most of the patrons were it not for the volume of the "OHHHHH" that followed any such drop and got everyone rubbernecking to see what had happened.

In fact, one group of guys from one of the nearby auto plants (they were all white collar workers), had witnessed so many of Stacy's "Whoops" that they decided to take precautionary action. On a pre-determined day, so as to head disaster off at the pass, they all came wearing rain coats. They were not disappointed by Stacy's reaction, which was heard 'round the world. Neither was the rest of the crowd.

Stacy filled in for one the girls one Saturday night. The evening was ripe for a little prank. Just a little background: At this point in time, we were still washing the bar glasses by hand, behind the bar, in the three little sinks, with the spinning brushes and the soap packet for sink number one. In sink number two was the plain rinse water, and in sink number three was a rinse agent. After a while, all this soap, water, and rinse agent took a toll on your hands, and your skin turned the same texture as sand paper, so we keep a pair of rubber gloves back there for the not so bold. ALSO...the waitri are expected to help out with the bar glasses every now and then.

Sooooo...as Stacy was getting ready to leave; it was time for us to put our plan into action that we had cooked up about ten minutes ago. As she was walking into the kitchen, I asked her to help with one more rack of glasses. She moaned and protested a little, but we knew she would cooperate. After all, she was a good sport. AND--this is VERY important--Stacy ALWAYS wore the rubber gloves. So, I, the boss, all customers at the bar, a couple of cooks, the busboys, and the waitri were all trying to inconspicuously hover about. Stacy reached for the gloves...the crowd tensed and held their breath.....she was pulling on the first glove and "OOOOOOOOHHHHH!!! What the hell is that?! Oh of...I'm not doing this. What's in there?! What are you looking at? Why is everyone standing around? Did you all know?! That was disgusting! It felt like UUGGGHHHHH!! Oh jeeeezzz...." Her eyes were open almost as wide as her mouth as she continued to react to the as yet unknown substance in the gloves. Everyone but Stacy knew that right before she came around the corner, we had filled the gloves with whipped cream.

Stacy reacted with more flare and volume than we had hoped for. Thus we have ended Act One that Saturday Night.

On any given Saturday night, the waitri would come wandering in at a staggered pace. One of the sister acts was working this evening, and as they were waiting for the rush to begin, they were standing around by the cigarette machine, talking. I was doing my best to get their attention to say "Hello," but it was to no avail. They just weren't paying attention. I did the next best thing. I wrote a note to send over to them via one of the other girls. It simply read, "Are the Snot Sisters too good to say hello?"

The waitri with the note walked the ten feet, or less, (I told you they weren't paying attention) and handed them the note. They both laughed when they read it and realized there was a ring of truth to it when I explained that I was trying to say "Hi" and they wouldn't turn in my direction. However, one of them did take to calling me the "Snot-tender" for the rest of the time she worked there.

A LITTLE LATER ON SATURDAY.....

Pretty soon it would be time for "Wheel of Fortune" to start. "Oh boy." Wait, let me say that one more time with more enthusiasm, "oh boy." Whoa...everybody rowdy down. The first puzzle is ready, and the players on the show are all drooling with excitement, as are a couple of people at the bar. After a few letters are turned, Patty, at the bar shouts out "Saturday Night Fever!!!" We all give her a deadpan look and in unison firmly say "NO!" There's no use in telling her she's not even close. She got the "Saturday" part correct, but that's it. After a few more letters are turned, Bob Whoever blandly says "Saturday Evening Post." We all know it's correct, but Patty refuses to give in until Vanna turns all the letters and we hear that annoying "Ding-ding-ding" sound.

Bob Whoever then asks what his prize is, so I throw him a packet of crackers. Patty is still pissing and moaning about being "almost right," so I throw her a packet of Sweet-n-Low and tell her not to eat it all at once.

Patty Duke and Grif are there, doing their usual thing. Patty Duke is talking to everyone; Grif is doing a crossword puzzle. Georgette and Harry are trying to stay awake. Dennis and Joan are having a liquid dinner, oh shit! Quick! Duck! Here come Cal and Anita!! Swiftly, I turn the corner and scurry into the kitchen. I peek out to see if the hostess has a table for them. Oh Please please please please please....YYYEEEEESSSSSSS! She has a table in the back of the dining room for them!! Oh happy day! Okay, now I can go back to work and make sure Georgette isn't ready to fall off the bar stool (she naps), and Bob (yes, another one) and Janine are ready to eat, like that's a big deal, the waitri are bothering me for drinks, someone wants their ashtray emptied and I tell them, "Quit smoking. That way it'll never get full. Besides that, you look like a cheap gangster the way you dangle that cigarette out of the corner of your mouth when you talk."

Her husband agrees with me.

The other Patty, not Patty Duke, is still trying to solve a "Wheel of Fortune" puzzle. "Hey Patty, you might be better at this game if you had learned how to read!" I toss her another packet of Sweet-n-Low. Hey, some people are easy.

YOUR HAIR LOOKS GREAT TODAY

If you want to absolutely assure yourself of getting a really good drink, all it takes is a few simple words. "Hey, your hair looks great today!" Be sure to say this with much enthusiasm.

There's always the chance that I may reply with, "So, you're saying all the other days it looked bad?"

"NO NO NO NO. It's just looking ESPECIALLY nice today!"

"Oh, okay, that's better."

It's important to know how to properly suck up. Some have even brought it up to an art form. They are proud of their sucking up skills, as well they should be. We often get a group of truck drivers who stop in when they are in town. As one was walking by the bar on his way to a table, you could hear him say, with much enthusiasm, "Hey, your hair's never looked better!!!" This would then be accompanied by a wink and a nod while never missing a step towards his table.

On one occasion, there was a new guy with one of the drivers, and he looked at the first guy, after he made this good hair comment, like he was nuts. He was heard to softly say (you gotta be careful, we hear everything), "What's her hair usually look like?"

"SSHHHH!! You wanna drink sludge the rest of the night? Just tell you like her hair, QUICK, before she pours our drinks!"

"But I don't understand. What's so great about her hair?"

Driver number one stopped, came back to the bar, and pleadingly said, "Please, you'll have to forgive him. He's just a rookie. He obviously doesn't know what he's saying."

"Alright, I'll cut you some slack. Just as long as you have him trained by the time you leave."

A little while later.....

"Hi, I'm Kyle. You'll have to excuse my rude behavior when we first came in. I guess I'm under a little stress, being the new guy on the block and all, but may I say that I don't think I've ever seen a more flattering hairdo than yours? You must spend hours getting ready, and we really appreciate it, after being on the road for days on end."

This kid's gonna be just fine.

"Hey Art! Nice job straightening the kid out. You do good work!"

There are times when one of the regulars may be in a frisky mood, wander in, and ask, "What happened to your hair today?"

"I tried to make it look like yours." Idiot.

Keeping your hair in place for nine hours takes work, and a bottle of industrial strength hair spray. Forget all those expensive brand names, just buy a gallon (you're gonna need a LOT), of whatever cheap crap your local drug store has on sale. Be sure to go past "Extra Superior Hold" and get "Wind Tunnel."

And don't even pretend to think you can get away with a hair-softening, ocean breeze and lilac scented, extra shine, body-enhancing, look-my-hair-is-gorgeous shampoo. My helmet of hair spray just laughs at frilly, gimmicky shampoos like that. The moment it makes contact with my hair, the hair spray just laughs and spits it into the bottom of the tub. Just about the only thing my hair has any respect for is Comet Cleanser.

You don't need anything to make your hair smell terrific is it would be a total waste of money. After being around cigarette smoke and all that cooking grease that gets absorbed by said hair spray, the only thing that's going to want to get close to your hair is a non-domestic animal.

You also don't need to worry about "shine." About a quarter of an inch of high lacquer content hair spray will reflect more light than you could ever get from the "natural shine" in your hair. Every now and then some fool will whine, "But that can't be healthy for your haiiiiirrrrrr." (Did you put some nasal tone in that whine?) I usually just give them a little head butt. When they get up off the floor, they can't remember what they were whining about.

I can't wait to tell them that I also belong to the "Color of the Month." OH, and just between you and me, not only am I a member of the Bad Hair Day Club for Women, I'm the president.

FASHION FAUX PAS

No one died and made me the Fashion Police. I appointed myself. But, my God, if you saw what some of these people were wearing, the first thing you'd say is, "Why didn't you start earlier?" The Importance of Wearing Matching Garments.

Hi Gary! You would think for a man with your education, you could learn to match the "Garanimals" tags a little better. Did you get dressed in the dark? Is everything else in the wash? Did you wake up and discover you no longer had any taste? It's a good thing you didn't have to accessorize or match a handbag. You don't have on two different shoes again, do you? At least you don't try to look like Carl."

THE IMPORTANCE OF LEAVING FASHION DECISIONS UP TO SOMEONE ELSE

"Oh hi, Carl! What's up? Did someone tell you biker black was gonna be popular this spring? If they did, they lied to ya, pal. Stick to blue jeans and polo shirts and you won't look like such a moron. Black is a bad color for you. It washes you out. Well, to be perfectly frank (or brutally honest), it makes you look dead."

It really doesn't matter what Carl wears, he'll still look like, well, Carl. You could put a freshly pressed tuxedo on him, and he would look like he just took a bath in it. It's also amazing. For having only half the hair that I do, it would take twice as much hair spray to tame that mess. And that's just what is growing out of his ears.

DRESSING LIKE A TRAMP: IT ISN'T FOR EVERYONE

"Hi Barb! What's happening? Did you have that shirt painted on? Or did you mean for the seams to be stretched out like that? Well, yes, that's a lovely shirt, if you're gonna stand out in the parking lot after dinner and try to turn a few tricks. Don't eat too much. We're not sure what the tensile strength of the thread holding that so-called shirt together is. I wouldn't want you to get embarrassed if you popped a seam. But then, I don't think you could get embarrassed just by virtue of the fact that you wore that thing out in public. If one of those buttons popped off, you could put someone's eye out. Where did you get it anyway, 'Tramps 'R Us?

"Okay, lovely chatting with you! Enjoy your dinner, talk to ya later!"

THE IMPORTANCE OF PROPER FOOTWEAR

"It's seventeen degrees out and snowing! I can't believe you have on open-toed, high-heeled hooker shoes!!! I can understand if you didn't watch the weather report, but did you look outside before you made your footwear selection? It's 10:00 at night. You had all day to see what the weather was like! You're going to get frost bite. You're not just gonna get frostbite on your feet either. If that skirt gets any shorter, you're gonna have a frost-bitten ass, too! Oh, I know, you're just going from the car to the door. What if you get stuck in the snow and have to walk? Not only will you get frost bite, you'll hit an icy patch and fall off of those four-inch, slut heels and break your ankle! THEN, your skirt will ride up during the fall, and your ass will get stuck to the ice!

"Does anybody know who that was?"

"It's my sister!" shouted one of the Bob's.

"Well now, that explains the lack of common sense."

Stupid, Stupid, Stupid.

THE TRICK IS WEARING THE COAT

I remember back in the nineties (I think it was) when some idiot started one of the most ridiculous fashion trends I have ever seen. Do you remember when high school kids, or those just slightly older, would wear their coats hanging off of their shoulders? It seems to me that that defeats most of the purpose of wearing a coat. This is Michigan, where we get sub-freezing temperatures far too often. So, here you've got these morons with their coats wide open and hanging off of their shoulders! They think it looks cool.

One of the girls was leaving work one night after we closed. I told her to button up her coat. It was only about twenty degrees outside. Her reply was, "OH! I'm sure! Do you know how stupid it looks to have your coat all wrapped around you?"

"Not as stupid as having it hanging off of your shoulders, thus causing the sleeves to be too long and the collar to bulge out in the back! Then it makes me wonder why you even brought a coat!!!"

Oh, for crying out loud, go look in a mirror and see what an imbecile you look like! (No offense meant to the imbeciles of the world.)

I told her, "Its 2:00 in the morning! There's no one out there to see you!" Anyone stumbling through the parking lot at this hour is seeing double anyways, so you can look twice as stupid.

She looked me like I had just arrived from Mars. Now I ask you, am I missing something here?

UNLESS IT'S A JACKET, MOST LEATHER SHOULD BE WORN BY NO ONE BUT THE COW

One of our looser-morals-than-most waitri came sauntering in one night sporting a leather skirt. Not only was it way too tight, it was wwaaaaaayyyyy too short. I might even go out on a limb here, and venture a guess that it was actually more than one size too small. I'm being kind. This skirt was so tight that if she had to pass gas and was seated at the time, she would launch herself straight up, just like a rocket.

The sausage-like roll of flesh that cascaded over the waistband were somewhat disguised by a not-large-enough

Hockey jersey. Now there's a fashion statement! I'm not sure what the statement is, but it's a statement. Since the fashion offender was mixing fashion genres, by which I mean the Sporty Look as exemplified by the hockey jersey and the Trampy Look as displayed by the "I think the cow is embarrassed" leather skirt, does that make her a Sports Slut? I here she is called her "Locker Room Lucy."

A LITTLE DAB WILL DO YA

One evening, one of the waitri was putting on some perfume in the restroom, which is very close to the end of the bar. When the door opened, we were enveloped in a cloud of perfume. I like perfume as much as anyone else, but I've always felt it should be something your sense of smell picks up on when you are in close proximity to the person wearing the perfume. You should not be able to smell it when they are in another room. AND you definitely should NOT be able to taste it in the air.

When this waitress approached the service bar, I kindly asked her, "What kind of perfume are you wearing?"

She excitedly replied, "Do you like it?"

"Yes, but in lesser quantities."

Sometimes subtlety is lost on people. On some it's more than sometimes. She continued, "Oh, is it a little strong?"

Again, I was kind with my response, "People can smell it in the parking lot, across town at the fertilizer plant."

LAUNDRY DAY

If you walk into the bar, and you hear the bartender, or anyone else for that matter say something to the effect of "Hey, Stan! How ya doin'? Must be laundry day, huh?" take a serious look at what you've got on. It can't be good. It's probably something a color blind tourist wouldn't be caught dead in, after his luggage got lost, and he borrowed clothes from Uncle Bob AND Aunt Myrtle.

Remember, it's the rest of us that have to look at you.

A couple of weeks later Stan came in sporting some plaid shorts that were unfashionably tight for any decade and a bowling shirt. "Hey, Bar Wench! How's does this look?"

"Stan, how many times do I have to tell you don't ask me a question you don't really want an answer to, you knuckle-dragging, mouth-breathing, four-eyed asshole?"

JELL-O

How do you get a bunch of grown men to act like little "Cosby kids?" (You don't have to do anything; they already do.) Simple, you pull out a Playboy magazine, open it to the centerfold, wait for lewd comments about where the staple is this month, and watch them start drooling. No, seriously, we can't do that here. Small children would walk by on their say to the salad bar and say "Oh look Daddy, they have the same magazine you keep hidden under the bed!" Busted!

No seriously, you settle for the next best thing. You serve these over-sized, eight year old morons Jell-O.

One Friday night, for no particular reason, I came into work armed with a couple of boxes of Jell-O. As soon as I got there, I went into the kitchen to get an empty sour cream container (All restaurants have these. They are the commercial equivalent to you saving a margarine tub to use as Tupperware.). I then poured in the two packages of red Jell-O, which were not the same flavor, because I KNOW someone out there is wondering that, and then added the hot water and stirred VERY THOUROUGHLY. If it's one thing I can't stand, it's grainy Jell-O. (I KNOW you know what

I'm talking about. You're sitting there eating Jell-O, and happy and shit, and then hit you a mouthful of Jell-O that has the texture of sand, and your first reaction is "Which one of you dumb fucks doesn't know how to stir Jell-O thoroughly?!?!?!? Then it dawns on you that you are eight years old, and if you said that to your mother, or one of your aunts, you'd be eating soap instead of Jell-O, so you just kind of keep that thought to yourself.) Then I added the cold water, did some more stirring, and then put it in the cooler.

Those at the bar were wondering what I was doing, so I told them not to worry about it because the Jell-O wasn't going to be ready on their shift. I told them they were not special, and they were not getting any special treats.

One of the Bob's started to whine, "But what if..."

"I SAID NO!"

"But..."

"NOOOOOO. Go play in traffic."

Fast forward about seven hours and "It's Jell-O time!"

OH HOOOORRRRAAAAYYYY!!!!

We had about six or seven guys at the bar. So I and Niki, the waitress who was working with me, told all the guys, in a lilting, sing-song manner, "We've got a suuuurrrpiiiiiise for you!" Their half bloodshot eyes opened up REAL wide. Then we told them to remain seated and keep their hands on the bar at all times.

"Bob, if you take your hand off of the bar, I'm gonna tell

everyone you're playing pocket poker."

We got out some monkey dishes, you know, like the ones they serve veggies or applesauce in, and then we pulled out the whipped cream. Again, we had to tell everyone to remain seated, keep their hands on the bar, and their mouths shut, for now. Finally, with much pomp and circumstance, we brought out the Jell-O! It was all regal and shimmery. (That's a combo of shiny and shimmer.) It had that subtle, sensuous movement to it, and it was the color of glorious, four-inch, red, patent leather high heels. Some call this color Bordello Red. I call it mixed fruit.

You wouldn't believe the looks on their faces. It was pure joy!!!

"WOW! I can't remember the last time I had Jell-O!!" (Some of these guys can't remember the last time they got laid.)

We called the boss up from downstairs and told him we had dessert for everyone. (He's got the biggest sweet tooth in this part of the state.) He came around the corner. "What have we-- OOOHHHHH." We gave him a dish of Jell-O, and he clutched onto it like a small child afraid the dog would come and take it from him. He climbed up on a bar stool, joined the other kindergarteners at the bar, and commenced shoveling in the JELL-O. He was also the first one to ask for seconds.

They all sat there like wide eyed little urchins who had never had a treat before. And they were quiet. It was truly a Kodak/Cosby moment. The little orphans in "Annie" could not have been more appreciative.

After the initial "AAHHH" factor wore off, everyone, including Niki and me, started to play with the JELL-O.

"I used to make a JELL-O volcano with the whipped cream in the middle."

"I like to mush mine up with the whipped cream and make it look like tomato soup!"

"OOOOH...you're sick."

"I like to squish mine through my teeth. WATCH!"

"NO!"

"Watch this! I like to..."

"BOB!!! Get your fingers out of the bowl. This is a utensil-only food!" Kids!

Then someone broke the magic spell and asked what flavor it was.

"What are you blind, you moron?!? It's red!"

"Good, 'cause I don't like strawberry."

Don't ask.

Since this went over so well, next week we'll open up the "Jell-O Wrestling Pit."

This brings us to Gravy Wrestling. This is much brought up topic with the late crowd. Every so often, some asshole says, "We should have mud wrestling here! I'd play! Throw in a couple of waitresses, and I'll jump right in!" If I've told them once, I've told them a hundred times. This is getting tiring. Here we go...

"Hey you! Missing Link! How many times do I have to tell you this is a roast beef place. If we're gonna have any wrestling at all, it's gonna be GRAVY WRESTLING!!!!!"

OTHER THINGS WE LIKE TO DO WITH THE LATE NIGHT CROWD....

One night, when Helen ran out to her car for a minute, (she was down to one pack of cigarettes and had to get a back up), we tried locking her out, but you can only keep the door locked on an open bar for so long before the boss gets a wee bit irritated. Actually, it's better if he doesn't find out at all, and if he sees all her cigarette smoke coming in under the door, he's going to think a waitress is outside on a self-declared cigarette break outside. Oh sure, he'll hear plenty of noise and cussing coming from Helen through the door, but the boss is used to that.

Since we couldn't keep Helen out for long that way, we went to the next best thing. We made a NO HELEN sign. You know the signs that have the red circle with the diagonal line through the object in the middle of the sign. Like the NO SMOKING sign has a picture of a lit cigarette. We replaced that with the word HELEN. We would've put a picture of Helen, but no one who was in on this had any drawing talent whatsoever. (No one had one of those stupid fucking phone cameras either. It hadn't been invented yet. Only James Bond had one of those) So, we opted for spelling out her name.

It's not that we don't like Helen. (We have to, or she'll hit us.) She's one of our favorites. It just happened to be her turn to get picked on. Remember, we are an equal opportunity bar; we give everyone a hard time.

So now that its only minutes before the end of the afternoon shift that Helen works, and we go out and tape the sign to the door. About two minutes later a stranger comes in and asks, "Who is Helen, and why don't you want her in here?"

We all started laughing, and saying, "Alright, cool, that worked. At least we know the sign can be clearly understood." At least it will be understood by most people with least some grasp of the English language. There's always going be some idiot who's gonna say, "I don't get it," and then he will stereotypically scratch his head. That will be after the explanation.

"Yeah, no mistaking that message."

Needless to say, he looked at us like we were...well, actually we don't care. He was new. We all stared back like children of the corn. It didn't scare him away. He sat down, ordered a drink, and we explained that we were doing this just for the sheer joy of annoying Helen, and waiting to see what her reaction would be.

We didn't have to wait ver....BOOM! The back door flew open and in came Helen! A giant poof of cigarette smoke proceeded all five feet and maybe one inch of Helen, full of spit and vinegar. (Helen never disappoints). It's a big door for such a little woman to be flinging open like it was an old wobbly screen door with no life left in it. AND she did it one-handed because in the other hand she was flailing about the "No Helen" sign! (The cigarette was dangerously dangling from her lips)

"ALRIGHT!!! Which one of you assholes put this sign on the door?!?!?" she barked LOUDLY, sounding like a pit bull who had just gotten bitten in the ass by a Chihuahua and looking like a dragon with the smoke coming out of her mouth. I swear, if you looked real hard, you could see the smoke coming out of her ears.

"I'm not gonna ask who made it because I know none of you can even draw a stick person, much less a straight line! It's gonna take more than a stupid little sign or a locked door to keep me out!!!"

As Helen walked the length of the bar, eyeing everyone there like a detective looking at a line-up, she hit everyone upside the head with the sign. Anyone named "Bob" she hit twice. Everyone was happy. The crowd got the reaction they were looking for, Helen knew she gave a good performance and would probably drink for free that night, and the stranger got a show he wasn't expecting.

"Hey, Bar Wench," Helen called out, "do you mind if take this sign home and have it laminated?"

F.Y.I.: Throughout the entire ordeal, Helen never lost the two and a half inch ash on her cigarette.

KEEBLER ELVES…ALL OVER THE BAR

Every now and then, the crowd gets a good one in on me. It's especially funny when they are ALL in on it. (It's always nice to know they did some planning. Now I can put "Plays well with others" on their report cards.)

I arrived for work the usual time one Friday, walked behind the bar, started to say "Hi" to everyone, and I noticed some snickers and giggles. (And that was from the men.) Some were sporting an anxious smile. Some were trying to hide the fact that they had a mouthful of something. Please, no "Chew and Show." I can't believe I have to remind some of these Neanderthals about that. Subtle, this crowd is not.

Then, I noticed a little Keebler Elf cookie sitting on the bar ledge in front of me.

"OOOOHHHHH! WOW!!! The Keebler Elf was busy this week!" I'm gonna bite, and humor them… You do know that I'm talking about Keebler, the short woman and the bar, not the elves that make the cookies. There's no such thing as elves, you dweeb. Of course Keebler and her sidekick were now howling with laughter. I hoped neither one of them had to pee, they could really embarrass themselves. The rest of the bar was starting to join in. Little did I know, this was just going to be the beginning. Not only was there a little Keebler Elf cookie sitting on the bar ledge in front or me, there was a little Keebler Elf cookie sitting on the bar ledge in front of everyone! They had them all propped up and standing tall! They looked like little cookie guards.

When I realized everyone had one, except for Vern, I asked him where his little elf cookie was. His chewing was the answer to that question, along with the crumbs on his chin and in his beer. "How many cookies have you had?!?"

In true grown up fashion, he held up six fingers. Five on one hand, the middle finger of the other.

I happened to look up at Virginia just in time to tell her, "Stop licking that elf like that! Not everyone wants to know how you make extra money!"

As I started to actually do some work, I went to pour a beer, and there were more little elf cookies, proudly staring at me from the top of the beer taps.

"Hey look at this!" I said, while pointing at the beer taps. The crowd roared again! Don't be so smug, if you were there you would have been right in the fray. The bartender who worked the shift before me was obviously in on this.

Then I found some little elf cookies standing guard in front of some of the liquor bottles.

This was starting to look a little ominous; I think these

elves had little elfin pitchforks.

Theeeennnn....when I opened up the cooler, I saw there were more elves, defiantly standing in front of the beer bottles. (They were so defiant, they looked like they had their little elfin arms crossed, daring me to reach in and take a bottle of beer. They had no weaponry, but they were baring their teeth like they were ready to bite.)

I thought I had found them all, then I went to make a blended drink, and there they were, keeping watch over the blender.

When one of the waitri at the service bar started giggling, I knew I had to look around there, too. Not to disappoint, they were protecting the straws and fruit swords. (I was momentarily worried that they might try to arm themselves with the little swords.) As I was about to cash out a customer, I heard a voice in the crowd say, "It's about time you opened the drawer," and there were more sitting on top of the quarters and dimes. Oh no!

The elves were looking meaner by the minute. I think the ones by the blender had bandoliers of bullets draped over their shoulders and were carrying little elfin machine guns. (I should have smoked one before I came in today.)

I finally picked one up and did what any self-respecting bartender would with a Keebler Elf cookie. I bit the head off. It broke the spell, they were all just cookies again, and I was no longer looking for illegal substances.

If this had been a Hitchcock story, it could have ended

verrrrrrrry differently.

GROVELING

There comes a time in everyone's life when they must grovel a little bit. That time came for Bob Who Spells it Backwards when he was in want of a cigarette. Bob Who Spells it Backwards comes in after work, which is usually around 10:00 p.m. We're not sure where he works or what he does and we don't particularly care. Nor have we ever bothered to ask. For a while now, Bob Who Spells it Backwards has been bringing in a lady friend. We're not really sure what the relationship is, and again, we don't really care. But there are times when we think he should just be a little nicer to her. The opportunity to present that point of view came up one night when Bob, you should know the routine by now, made a stupid comment to me. No one can remember the exact comment, it was stupid, and that's all that matters.

I believe it had something to do with smoking because I reached out and took his lighter as he was about to light up a cigarette. He thought he could hold out, but it wasn't long before a nicotine urge prevailed upon him. He asked, "May I have my lighter back, please?"

To which I replied, "No."

"Pretty please?"

"No."

"Pretty please with sugar on top?"

"No."

"What do I have to do?" he pleaded.

"Grovel."

"But I was groveling," he protested.

"Not enough."

"Pretty please with sugar on top and a dozen roses on the side?"

"You know what Bob? You need to grovel to her," I said as I pointed to his lady friend.

He looked at me with an incredulous blank stare, like I had just asked him to take a bath in acid.

"C'mon Bob, you can do it."

That look was still on his face.

His lady friend was smiling sweetly, waiting for the groveling to begin. Then Bob desperately blurted out, "I'll grovel to you for thirty minutes!"

"Won't work Bob, you have to grovel to her," as she was still sweetly smiling.

"But...but...but..."

"Bob, stop mumbling. You sound like more of an idiot then we already think you are."

So, then Bob looked at her and opened his mouth, but no sound would some out.

"How bad do you want that cigarette, Bob?"

Bob was thinking he could hold out longer, but he couldn't. He was seriously cracking. It was really a simple solution. The rest of the bar was even telling him, "C'mon Bob. It won't kill you to say something nice to her."

But alas, Bob was truly perplexed. For some reason known only to him, he just could not bring himself to grovel to the designated grovellee. (That's another one of those words) THEN! Thinking he's clever (not the first mistake), he sees that Quiet Mike, who's sitting to his left, has just lit a cigarette and asks if he can borrow his lighter. Without missing a beat, Quiet Mike picks up his lighter, puts it in his pocket, and tells Bob, "Nope, I'm not finished drinking yet."

Bob then puts on a disgusting display as he begs for a light. Quiet Mike tells him he's groveling to the wrong person. Bob had that desperate pleading look on his face. I looked over at him and barked, "For cryin' out loud Bob, stop whimpering, you pansy! Be a man and grovel!"

Of course, it didn't help that Helen was sitting to the left of Quiet Mike, smoking like Mt. St. Helen's in mid-eruption. I picked up a menu and tried to fan some in Bob's direction.

"Breath deep, Bob. You know what they say. Second-hand smoke is better than no smoke at all…. Bob, would you like to go in the kitchen and sniff a broiler?"

Suddenly Bob perked! "You mean the burners are still on????"

"No, you fool, I was just going to turn the gas on let you sniff the propane."

The next thing you know, Bob is trying to rub two toothpicks together. Idiot.

"Knock that off Bob, the only thing you are going to get by doing that is a splinter, and no one here is going to help you get it out, unless I get a carving knife from the back. Bob!!! Stop it! If the Fire Marshall comes in you're gonna be in big trouble!!!"

We're not sure, but we think Bob may have incurred some brain damage from the sudden nicotine withdrawal. Most people will never notice. Bob resigned himself to nicotine depravation. He never did get his lighter back. (Grow some balls, Bob) It was a much longer night for Bob than it was for the rest of us. Heh-heh.

Just a quick aside about cigarettes, I quit smoking years ago, so now I have no sympathy for smokers. When they ask if we have a cigarette machine, I tell them "NO" (it was removed after the boss decided it took up too much room) and then start laughing. They may think I am a tad rude. When they ask if there is one in the lobby of the hotel behind us, I start laughing harder and answer. "No." THEEENNNNN......when they ask where is the nearest place to get cigarettes; I start laughing even HARDER and tell them they have to go to the gas station at the corner. It's only about a quarter of a mile. HAHAHAHAHA

About the time they started making all those laws about where you could and couldn't smoke, I figured I'd better quit, or I would end up having a real attitude problem. I smoked for twenty years and then quit. I earned the right to laugh. So, to all who whined, screw you!

THE CUSTOMER IS ALWAYS RIGHT (N O T !)

"The customer is always right" is one of the most worn out, over-used, pull-it-out-of-your-ass expressions that still circulates in the world of commerce. Whoever (the name escapes me at the moment) coined that phrase was NOT dealing in a situation where alcohol was involved.

People always seem to blurt out that phrase when they know they haven't got a leg to stand on. For instance, (I'm glad you asked), you go into a grocery store, you pile up $150.00 worth of food in your cart, and then proceed to tell the cashier that this food is only worth $100.00, and that's all you are going to pay. Do you really expect the cashier to say, "Okay, you're the customer? You're right!"? Not in this lifetime, and not on this planet!

I love it when people blurt out "I'm the customer, and I'm right!"

"You're right. You are the customer."

"And I'm right!!"

"Right, left, let's not discuss politics."

"I'm not talking about politics. I'm the customer!"

"You're right. You're the customer."

"And I'm right!!"

"Okay and Bob is sitting to your left, which would be my right."

"NO!!! I'm right!!!"

"You will ALWAYS be right to those sitting on your left, no matter where you are."

"NNOOOOOO! I'm saying I AM right!"

"Hi, Right, I'm Gretchen."

"Oh, forget about it, can I just have another beer, please?"

If you were wondering what Mr. Right was so adamant about being right about, it doesn't matter, he can't remember, and you should know the drill by now, "I don't care."

WHAT TO DO WHEN RELATIVES COME IN THE BAR

You do nothing. After all, these people know you better than anyone sitting at the bar. You treat them in the same gnarly fashion you treat everyone else. If I didn't, some would ask "What's your name and what have you done with Gretchen?"

There ARE circumstances that do call for a little action. Such as the time I told everyone that Dan and Janice were my cousins. It wasn't long before some inquiring minds wanted to know which one of them was related to me. I have to tell you I was a wee bit irked when they pointed at each other and simultaneously said "her/him."

"Dan, don't make me tell stories from our youth."

"Gretchen, why would you want to embarrass Janice?"

"I'm talking about when YOU were a kid!"

"But I didn't meet you until I was twenty-seven."

"Dan, we were babies together!"

"Well, technically we were, due to the close proximity of our ages, but we were babies together in different parts of the country."

"You are so full of it!!!"

A voice came from a few seats down, "Yeah, they're cousins alright. He argues just like her, and if he weren't related to her, there would be no reason to argue the point this long."

Dan looked down the bar and asked, "What really gave me away?"

"When we first asked which one of you was related to her," he said nodding in my direction, "Vern walked by and pointed at you. On his return trip from the restroom, he said he had met you before."

"Thanks, Vern. You're a real pal." That was Dan, and I think he was a wee bit sarcastic.

Vern replied, "Beer talks, and they were buying." You just can't argue with logic like that. Dan just shook his head in defeat. He thought for sure everyone would think that Janice was the relative, as she and Vern sang, yet again, their rendition of the theme song from the old television show, "Green Acres."

SMALL CHILDREN

When relatives bring in their small, adorable children for dinner, it's the children who get the royal treatment. I think all small children are adorable, but I am particularly biased when they are small, adorable children who happen to be hanging upside by their knees on a branch of my family tree.

When Cassie would come in with her parents, my cousins (I have a LOT of cousins), I would run over to front, where they were standing, waiting to be seated, and take Cassie behind the bar with me. I would promptly introduce her to crowd as my new assistant. Everyone would ooh and ahh, and you could hear all the "Oh my, she is so cute" comments. I would reply, "Of course she's cute. She's related to me."

Anyone with a rude rebuttal to that comment was forced to hold it in. After all, there was a small child standing next to me. Ha ha.

With her head tilted back, Cassie would gaze up at everyone. (She wasn't much taller than the sink) and behold a sea of smiles. Then we would walk down to the service bar, and I would give her a couple of maraschino cherries on a pretty, colored, "sword" toothpick. With toothpick firmly clenched in hand, now all sticky with cherry juice, I would deliver her back to her parents.

Everyone would wave bye-bye as Cassie went off to her table to have dinner, thinking she was queen for a day.

Then some clod has to break the magic spell the adorable

child has momentarily cast upon the bar, with a stupid comment, like, "I'm surprised she doesn't run away when she sees you."

"You'll pay for that, Vern."

Why would she run and scream? She knows she's going to get a treat, like the cherries on a special sword. At home, I give them candy.

As the years sped by, Cassie got to be nine or ten years old and developed a shy streak and no longer wanted to come back behind the bar, so the "next generation" had to take her place. Enter Annie.

Annie boldly marched behind the bar upon her arrival and looked up at everyone with a challenging gaze (gotta love this kid) as if daring them to stop her from getting her cherries on a special sword. After watching Annie for a minute, one of the patrons asked, "Are all the small children in..."I had to interrupt her, "WHOA! The proper phrasing of that question would be, "Are all the small, ADORABLE children..." You may continue. She started over again, "Are all the small, adorable children in your family blond?"

"Yes, it's a rule."

YOUR DATING LIFE BECOMES ENTERTAINMENT FODDER FOR THE BAR

If you're going to spend your life insulting people, you've got to give a little of yourself back, or you will forever be looking behind you trying to see what's going to bite you in the ass. I've found it's always best to make fun of yourself before anyone else can. And, of course, immediately turn around and make fun of them again. So throughout this whole process, I shared my dating life with them.

"I don't know if I would be bragging about that, Bar Wench!"

"Shut up, Vern. At least I HAVE a dating life!"

At one point in time, I dubbed myself "The One Date Wonder." (If I left it up to the crowd, or Vern, the nickname could have been a lot ruder.) I handled it in a good humored fashion, but the moniker was true. Not only did some of these guys never call me again, they didn't even show up at the bar anymore!

One guy came to a barbecue at my house and brought his son, who was the same age as my son, and most of the other kids there. Everyone had a great time! We ate, we drank, we threw toys back in the pool every time the kids threw them out. The weather was picture perfect. What more could you ask for? This guy even called after he got home! WOW! And then, I never heard another word. He even disappeared from the bar/restaurant, city, and the face of the earth...

Next guy. He worked the afternoon shift at one of the auto plants (big surprise there) and used to come in for lunch a lot. "Used to" being the operative words here. I thought he looked interesting. So, one Sunday we went to lunch. It was a nice time. We had a nice conversation.

I never heard another word. He disappeared from the bar/restaurant, city, blah, blah, blah.

I thought a pattern was starting to develop, and if it continued, people might begin to notice the crowd was thinning.

Pretty soon, the close, intimate group of thirty or forty that I shared my dating life with, were now asking, "Scare anyone off this week?"

"What did you do to these guys?"

"This might be a good way to get rid of the customers you don't like."

"Hey, Broadzilla, who's your next victim?"

I figured I just had to find a tougher specimen.

Next. This was someone I had known for quite a while, so we went out, had a good time, yada yada, yada.... You know the drill. He actually talked to me after that, but then about a week later, he told me he was getting back together with his old girlfriend. Another one bites the dust. (I don't think there was an old girlfriend.)

Did I give up?!? NO!!! I endeavored to persevere! I had a bar crowd to entertain.

The close intimate group of thirty or forty started to number the men I dated.

One of the regulars that I had known for eons told me one night he wanted to be number fifty-two, since that was his age at the time. He also requested that I let him know when I got to number fifty, so he would have time to get ready, but promised that he would NOT stop coming to the bar.

There are a few more on the list, (a lot), but really, who wants to keep counting the duds, unless of course it's to keep the crowd amused.

Since there was a hotel behind us, (stop that thought right now, you nasty minded piece of trash) we got a lot of out-of-towners, most of whom were here for business. Some were here for months at a time. Since I did on occasion date people from many of the other forty-nine states, I did consider myself to be part of the "national dating scene." (It's okay if you choked on that last comment. I even rolled my own eyes back as I was writing it.)

For a while, I was thinking of starting a business to help separated couples get back together. I could contact the wife, and if she wanted to get back together with her husband, all she had to do was get him set up an a date with me, and he'd come running back. I had no real explanation for why this happened. Maybe it's just a gift.

I decided not to pursue this venture, as it could have been just a little too much for my ego to handle. But then, if I had, then I could have written a book about how to handle rejection, with real life situations and how to handle them, with all the info right from the horse's mouth: *Been There, Done That, Dated it, Moved On* subtitled *Over and Over and Over and Over Again, and Then Some.*

Although…Number Three (with the old girlfriend story) did continue to come in the bar, he never came in by himself. He always had his buddies with him. To really break the pattern (at this point in time, I think I was up to number eight or nine), we did go out one other time. It was a couple of years later, the restaurant was closed for two weeks for remodeling, and I had a Friday night off. So, we had been talking about shooting pool, and we decided this would be a good night to go. He suggested we go to dinner also. Okay.

So there we were eating dinner, and I made a comment about Little Billy, the cook, I said, "I think Little Billy is scared of me." Bachelor Number Three, without missing a beat, a movement of his fork, or a bite of his meal, replied, "A lot of people are scared of you."

AHA! I thought. So are you! Knowledge truly is power. Heh-heh. Then I humored myself with the thought that when I got older, I was gonna be one of those "Tough ol' broads." I like that.

Heh-heh. (Someone else told me I was gonna be one whacked-out ol' lady and that I should start collecting cats right now. I only have one cat at the present. My son told me it was my starter cat. At least they're on the same page. I, um, haven't read that one yet.)

So what do you do when scaring 'em off one at a time gets old? You go for two at a time!!

One of these gentleman was again, someone I had known for quite a while, who was separated from his wife. Okay, I know what you're saying, "She has got to know this isn't going anywhere." And you're right, but then it's not always the destination, sometimes it's the journey.

This guy was a friend of a friend. They worked at a place across the street (which was not an auto plant, go figure), and it was convenient for them to come to the bar after work. They also used to have their company Christmas party here.

The friend that this guy was a friend of--are you following me, or does everyone have to have a name? Alright, so it's Jason, just to keep things simple, and we'll call his friend, Tim. So Tim starts coming in more and more often with Jason, for dinner (Remember, Jason ate there three to five times a week.) because he (Tim) was no longer eating diner at home.

One night, the conversation got around to music. You know how those conversations go.

"Yeah, I play the piano," I admitted.

"You should have been at the Billy Joel--What's his name

concert."

"Yeah, that would have been a good one."

"Blah blah. "Blah blah blah."

"Have you been to the symphony?" "Not in a long time."

"Want to go?"

"Sure."

"Okay, find out a schedule and pick a day."

"Okay." I was a little surprised. This guy was not your typical symphony material. He was in trucking. Trucking scrap metal.

I called the Detroit Symphony Orchestra and had them send me a schedule. (This was pre-internet). I see a concert that sounds interesting, so the next time Tim is in the bar, I show him the schedule. He says the day I want to go is fine, to pick out any tickets I want, and let him know how much they are. There are a lot of variances in the prices, anywhere from thirty dollars to eighty dollars. He says anything is fine, but I may want to stay away from the eighty dollar seats. Sounds reasonable to me.

Jason and Tim are the only two at the bar. There's a football game on, and all's right with the world. In comes Mach. Hey! When did he get here, about two weeks ago, wasn't it? Helen won the bet. Actually Helen always wins the bet, but all those morons she bets with haven't figured it out yet. They think she is very intuitive. Turns out he was very pleasant to talk to, stare at, and lust after. Oh yeah, and interesting, too.

Last Sunday I took him to a local gym and then we went to

Greenfield Village, which is a local tourist attraction, It's like going back in time to the way life was in the early nineteen hundreds. Anyway, I figured since Mach was only in town for a couple of months, it would be safe for my ego when he left to go home because it wouldn't be my fault. And it's also my birthday, and I thought it was a pretty gutsy move when he came in and gave me a coffee mug that made fun of my hair. It said, "Bad hair day. Approach with caution." Some of the regulars thought he had a death wish.

What's that? You had no idea I was gonna hook up with Mach? No big surprise. You weren't paying attention, you weren't being observant, and I'm really smooth. So much for all being right with the world. You see, I knew Mach was coming in, but I thought it would have been earlier, when the bar was crowded, and he wouldn't be seated anywhere near Tim. But the crowd kept thinning until it got down to Jason and Tim.

So here comes Mach later than normal, and now you ask, "Why was he late?"

He was late because he was out getting the aforementioned coffee mug and wrapping it. I thought getting me a birthday present was very thoughtful, considering he hasn't been around too long. And....where, you ask, was he sitting? Well, he was two chairs down from Tim. There they were, all in a row, Jason, Tim, empty seat, and Mach. And me, standing on the other side of the bar, opening a birthday present, and just being the epitome of calm. Only on the outside. On the inside my stomach and colon were threatening mutiny and trying to send mostly digested food back up where it came from. Of course, I had to show Jason and Tim the coffee mug. They looked at Mach with a little bit of admiration and told him, "It takes a lot of guts to give her something that makes fun of her hair like that."

He just said (in East Coast fashion), "Well, whatta ya gonna do?"

Then, in true male fashion, they all turned their attention back to the football game. I breathed a sigh of relief. I went back to making twenty-five cent bets with Jason about the football game. "I'll bet you a quarter they won't get twenty yards in this possession."

"I'll bet another quarter this team will get a touchdown."

"Okay, this quarter says they won't get thirty yards on the kickoff return."

"It's 4 and 6. They won't make it."

This went on for the rest of the game. It kept all conversations neutral. I mean, it's one thing to date two guys at the same time, but you really don't want them in the same bar at the same time, much less sitting this close together. Ah, take a walk on the wild side.

At the end of the game, they were all getting ready to leave, and Tim asked for his and Jason's tab, but Jason beat him to it. After Jason paid, Tim looked up and said, "You can get those eighty dollar seats if you want to."

Tim and Jason went out the front door, and Mach went out

the back door. Whew.

A little while later, my buddy Number 52 came in and asked how my night was going and what number was I up to today. I said, "My night was interesting, and I'm on numbers ten AND eleven."

He said, "Sounds like there may be a story in there."

I got myself a fresh cup of coffee and sat down to have a chat.

"Hey guess what Little Billy did tonight?" I asked Number 52.

"Tried to become number nine?"

"No, but that was a good guess. His folks came in for dinner tonight, so he decided to freak them out a little. He told them his new girlfriend was here tonight and asked them if they would like to meet her. They were all thrilled and shit, and said that of course they would like to meet her. Little Billy came up to the bar and got Helen, complete with cigarette dangling out of her mouth, brought her over to their table, and introduced her as his new girlfriend."

Little Billy is about 22 years old, and Helen is not. Actually, Helen is real close in age to Little Jimmie's mom.

"Nice. What did the folks do?" Number fifty-two asked.

"They were truly in a state of panic, until everyone started laughing. Then his mother grounded him for almost giving his father a heart attack. But that really became a moot point when he reminded them that he didn't live with them anymore."

AFTERMATH

Let's fast forward a couple of weeks down the road.

It's symphony night. I traded my usual Saturday night shift for the Saturday day shift. About half an hour before I was to leave, Mach came in. I was chatting with him and asked him why he was limping. He said he'd hurt his foot, but wasn't sure how. We had decided earlier in the week that we would go to the gym again on Sunday. Blah, blah, blah, more conversation.

When it was time for me to leave, the rest of the customers starting clapping and were congratulating for having a date that evening.

"Hey hey hey!!!!!!... Have a good time! WINK WINK (how fucking subtle)... Try not to scare this one off... Way to go!!!!... Has he got health insurance?"

"You know, you guys are so cute I just want to squeeze your little cheeks until your balls fall off."

When everyone is applauding you and making comments, it's kind of hard to ignore. I really wish that Mach had not been a witness to any of this. So he asks me, "Why is everyone clapping?" I tell him to come outside with me for a minute, and I'll explain. While we were standing in the parking lot, I told him where I was going and that I NEVER take Saturday night off, so the crowd (outside of being rude ass holes) was a little happy for me and that I would see him tomorrow. Whew.

THEN... to add insult to injury, the bartender who took over for me came bounding out the door, thinking that Mach had walked out on his tab. I had to explain that he was just talking to me for a minute and would be back in.

Next week, I'm gonna have to explain to her why he wanted to talk to me. It never ends.

Later, it's off to the symphony. It's seems Tim is starting to feel a little uncomfortable. When we went to dinner afterwards, I could hear his stomach rumbling. It didn't sound like that "I'm hungry" rumble, more like an upset stomach rumble. (There is a difference) By the end of dinner, he said he felt like he had the flu. He was beginning to pale and look clammy. We finished dinner, went back to my house, he came in for a few minutes, and then left. He didn't look too good. Oh well, there's always tomorrow, the gym, and Mach.

The next morning, before I am supposed to meet Mach, he calls and asks where the nearest emergency room is. He says he can't even walk; his foot is so sore. I told him I would pick him up and drive him to the hospital. When we left the hospital, he was on crutches. Since going to the gym was out, we went to breakfast and then watched a lot of football.

The next time I was at work, the group was anxiously awaiting a report on my big "Two Date" weekend. I spit out, "One got the flu, and the other had to go to the hospital."

The crowd was all nodding in unison. "Nice to see you haven't lost your touch."

I could hear a murmur in the background. "And you

thought my health insurance question was out of line."

PEOPLE THAT CATCH OUR ATTENTION

FAMOUS SPORTS PERSONALITIES

One night, a verrrrry tall gentleman came in through the back door. (Remember, this door is right by the bar.) Well, it turns out that this gentleman is a professional basketball player. One of the waitri saw him first and recognized him. She discreetly pointed him out to me, which was good, because otherwise I had no idea who this guy was, and then we quietly told the guys at the bar. You want to talk about being Subtle?!? We can't! These guys were SO INCREDIBLY OBVIOUS! I found it extremely humorous that these so called men could so quickly turn themselves into a herd of "deer in the headlights."

"Hey, Jerry, I just put dog shit in your drink."

"Yeah, yeah, whatever…okay…aahhhhh…sure…"

"Hey Don, your shirt is on fire!"

"Okay, I'll get to it in a moment."

"Oh Briiiian, your wife is screwing another man in the phone booth!"

"Uh-huh, that's nice.…"

See what I mean? Complete morons.

As this very tall gentleman was walking back to his table, I thought all the guys at the bar were auditioning for parts in the next "Exorcist" movie. Until that point, I didn't know it was possible to actually turn your head THAT far around and not incur serious muscle damage. If there had been any chiropractors on the crowd, they would have been in heaven passing out business cards. You would have thought Lady Godiva just rode through with a fresh haircut. Even then, these fools would have waved her out of the way so they could watch this guy sit down.

Hey guys! Just a hint for future celebrity ogling, first do a chin check, and slap your mouth closed. That "mouth-hanging-open-stare" just is not conducive to being cool. At all. I don't know why I waste my breath. They're not cool anyways, and never will be.

A little while laterI pointed out, "Hey guys, I can't believe you were staring that hard at another man." They all came to attention at once.

"Do you know who that was?!?!"

I'll wait until they get both of their feet back on the ground before I point out to them that just because they were in the same building as greatness doesn't mean any of it is going to rub off on them. If I told them right now, the fall would be too much for some. However, this does give them bragging rights should they stop at another bar. I can hear it now...

"Yeah, just as he was coming through the door, he nodded

at me. I nodded back. It was cool." Oh, to live in their warped little world. The reason he nodded was so he wouldn't hit his head on the doorway.

PAUL NEWMAN

Rumor has it, one day Paul Newman came in for lunch. It seems he was with Jack Roush, from Roush racing. That makes sense. Roush Racing was located just around the corner. You don't expect too many famous people to just walk in off the street. The waitress who was lucky enough to have these gentlemen in her section gave them the exact same service she would give to anyone else in her section. She was cool, didn't stare or drool, or ask for an autograph. She didn't stutter when taking their order, or spill any food or drinks, due to nervousness from having an internationally known movie star at her table. The rest of the staff was really impressed with her composure. So was the boss. After all, she was rather young, and one would expect her to be at least a little star struck. But not her, she was as cool as a cucumber.

"Hey, Ashleigh! You're dong a great job on that table!"

"Whatever. A table's a table."

My eyes bugged out of my head. "Do you know who that is?!?!"

"Do I know who who is?" She was so damn bland about it all.

"That guy at your table! He's one of the most famous actors in the world!!!!"

"You mean the old guy with the gray hair?"

There's the secret to her calm demeanor. SHE DIDN'T KNOW WHO PAUL NEWMAN WAS!!!!!

"MY GOD CHILD, WHAT PLANET ARE YOU FROM!?!?!?! WERE YOU BORN YESTERDAY!?! HAVE YOU BEEN LIVING UNDER A ROCK!?!? WHAT DO YOU MEAN YOU'VE NEVER HEARD OF HIM?!?!? HAVE YOU NEVER SEEN A MOVIE?!?! WHAT?!? HE'S OLD!!!??? YOU'VE NEVER SEEN A PAUL NEWMAN MOVIE?! WHAT? BUT..."

Oh wow, do I ever feel old. No, no, I'm not old; she's just a moron.

FAMOUS ROCK GROUPS

Well, actually the heading should be Famous Rock Group. Singular. I just put the "s" after group to try and make you think we were a really cool hang out. We are, that is, the place IS a really cool hang out, if you're middle aged, give or take a couple of decades.

Alright, back to famous rock group(s). It was about 1978 or so, and a band was staying at the hotel behind us, and they came in late one night for a few drinks. Like I said, it was late, and no one else was in the restaurant, so they had the entire bar to themselves.

I learned an important lesson that night. Not all rock stars drink like fish. (Hey, I grew up in the early 70's. We all learned to self-medicate) After the first round, they were all ordering Piña

Coladas. The first to order a Piña Colada liked it so well, that he had the rest of them try it, and well, the rest is history. There I was serving Piña Coladas, which they renamed Killer Coladas, to "Canned Heat." If you're under 45, you probably don't remember them, but the important part is, I do. I was only about 22 years old at the time, so it was very cool to have a rock group at your bar, all to yourselves.

Before I realized who they were, we were just having your everyday, ordinary conversation. Then, when I found out who they were, we just continued our everyday, ordinary conversation. BUT WOW!!!!!! DID I HAVE BRAGGING RIGHTS!!! NA NA NA NAAAAAA NAAAAA!

LOCAL CELEBRITIES: WHO CARES?

Alright, who cares was a bit unfair, but I was also trying to see if you were paying attention. I have met some very nice local celebrities, and I have met some and thought, "I can't believe you're this big of a drunk."

Allow me to expound on that a little.

A local newscaster wandered in one afternoon. He was with a friend, and they were enjoying Happy Hour. At the end of Happy Hour, we always do a "last call" for Happy Hour. Well, this newscaster ordered last call for himself and his friend. I had to explain to him that his buddy had already left; yet, he insisted I put out last call for him. So I did. His friend was definitely not present. I had already cashed out his tab and watched him walk out the door. That was my first clue. The second was when he said "Goodbye." When the newscaster thought I wasn't looking, he picked up the drink of his buddy who was not there and downed it. Quickly. Very quickly.

What a lush!!! Good thing he wasn't doing the news that evening.

"Hey! Is it too late to get another Happy Hour round for me and my friend?"

And then there was the guy from one of the local appliance stores, who used to do his own commercials. He was a rude, cranky bastard. We never shopped at his appliance stores, so we won't waste anymore time talking about him.

The former hockey player turned sportscaster was a really nice guy. He was kind of quiet, very polite, and never gave anyone a hard time. You'd never believe he once played hockey.

But the frosting on the cake was the guy who did the local bowling show. It's hard to believe that anyone who was that BIG of a jerk could hold down the job that he had in television. Or was it that no self-respecting pseudo-celebrity would host that stupid of a show. Good ol' Bowling for Big Bucks Bennie Butthead.

THE ANNUAL GOLF OUTING

Let me start by saying, not only had I never put on a golf outing before, I had never even played in one! But why get hung up on the details. Before I even got started, I came up with a rule, "There will be NO priests in my golf outing."

You see, I used to play every Wednesday morning with a friend of mine, Rob. We would meet at the same golf course every Wednesday morning, and when we went into the clubhouse to pay, we would ask who we were paired up with this week. Well, on one particular Wednesday we were informed that we were paired up with Father Bill and Mr. Smith. Upon hearing this news, I quickly let an "Oh shit," slip out of my mouth, and just as quickly Rob elbowed me and told me to watch my language.

Sooooo....we got our stuff and got in line for the first tee, anxiously looked around for Father Bill and Mr. Smith. We proceeded to the first tee, Rob hit, and then we waved to the two guys behind us, who we assumed were Father Bill and Mr. Smith, but they just signal for us to go on ahead. Fine by us, we'll play as a twosome.

At the end of the round, we talk to couple of rangers, one

of whom informs us that Father Bill waved us on because he doesn't play with women. Yeah, that sat real well with me. BUT, to add insult to injury, a couple of weeks later, I show up at the golf course, and there are no cars in the parking lot, so naturally I wonder what is going on. I find out the course is closed for the day for an outing put on by the Bishop. Bumped off by priests again! And you thought my rule was harsh!

Alright, this is a golf outing. For a bar. It's gotta be stupid! Right down to my stupid little poem, which I AM going to make you suffer through. (I make the rules, remember?) These are not golfers who happen to drink; these are drinkers who happen to golf. Drinking is what they all have in common. It's not like everyone subscribes to the New England Journal of Medicine, and at the weekly meeting they discuss things like the latest in chemo-therapy. No, the closest they get to discussing medicine is reminiscing about the different methods of "self-medicating" they, like I, learned in the 1970's or what they thought the best hangover cure was. The closest they might get to all reading the same magazine would be "MAD" magazine. But that would only start endless and pointless debates about Spy vs. Spy. Don't ask me about this, just go buy a magazine.

The big discussion amongst all the players before the big outing wasn't who could drive the farthest or who could putt like there was no tomorrow. No, it was more along the lines of, "Hey, what are you gonna bring to drink?"

"Well, Jim and I are going to get there early, so we can get a parking spot right along the back nine. That way, when we run out of beer, I can slowly drive the cart along the edge of the parking lot while Jim grabs more beer from the reserve cooler in the car."

"Whoa, good plan! I was thinking of bringing a pint of Schnapps as a back up."

"Dave lives near the course, and he said he was going to go out the evening before and hide a cooler in the woods along the fourth fairway."

"Betty is bringing a bottle of rum and some Coke. Hey, Betty, how are you going to fit all those bottles of Coke in the cooler?"

Betty looked over the top of her reading glasses (she was perusing the menu) at the moron who just asked her that question and said, "I don't need much Coke."

Okay, enough about the booze. Here's my stupid poem (I warned you) to set the mood for the golf outing. (If you say this poem in the same rhythm you would use for "Twas the Night Before Christmas," you'll get through it just fine.)

Just read the damn poem!

TWAS THE NIGHT 'FORE THE OUTING
(No pun intended on "fore.")
Twas the night 'fore the outing, and up at the bar,
The golfers were gathered from near and from far.

They checked on their tee times, to see when to start,
They spoke of the beer they would haul in their cart.

Today all the skies had decided to drain,
It was a regular deluge of rain.
Many would worry when the sun would shine next,
Not me, I was certain golf day would be blessed.

(It better be, I'm not giving refunds)

As the dawn slowly broke, the skies were bright blue,
All the clouds were now gone, except for a few.
All in their carts, patiently waiting in line,
It now seemed that everything this day would be fine.

On Donnie and Ronnie and Leo and Dave!
Don't crash that cart! Please try to behave!
We know you've been drinking since day before last,
All hopes of your winning have surely been dashed.
Here comes "Crashin' Carrie," Oh who let her drive?
Her partner is surely glad to just be alive.
Carrie should stop having drinks as her meals.
Look out everyone! She just lost a rear wheel!

No one this day deemed to have any sense,
One tossed his club, got it stuck in a fence.

Another decided to drive through a creek,
A new group of golfers, I think I shall seek.

Okay, thank you for letting me get that out of my system. I'm all done with my poem, but I swear, all of it is true! C'mon, tell me the truth. You want more, don't you? When playing in a golf outing, don't ever go first, if you can help it. Everyone watches! Seeing as how it was technically my golf outing since I put it all together (and made up the rules), it just seemed natural that I be the first to tee off. I wasn't feeling very natural about it. I'm a lousy golfer. But I got up and gently placed the ball on the tee, stepped back and looked at the fairway (I was stalling for time), made a couple of practice swings, took a deep breath, got into position, swung the club back, and lo and behold, made contact with the ball!!! Not very good contact, mind you, but I did hit it! It must have gone upwards of forty or fifty yards! Oh, come on and give me a break! Forty of fifty yards in a football game would be quite impressive.

Okay, maybe the ball didn't travel very far, but it sure made a nice straight line in all the grass it plowed through. Did I fail to mention that it did not get up in the air either? I was just being a good hostess and trying to make sure that everyone else felt better about their own golfing skills.

The best part about my less than impressive drive is that it didn't matter. This outing is a "Scramble." That means that all four members of a team hit, then you collectively decide which was the best drive, and the entire team then hits from that spot, picking up all the other balls along the way. The only way my team would ever use one of my drives was if by some freak of nature, all three simultaneously broke both their arms and had to swing the club buy holding it in their mouth. Even then, the chance of using one of my drives is only fifty-fifty.

In this "Scramble" mode, every shot works the same way. We all hit the second shot and moved on to the best shot, picking up the other balls along the way. The best chance of using one of my shots is on the green, providing someone hit it within two feet of the hole, the wind is moving with me, there are no shadows on the green, and when no one is watching, I can pick it up and drop it in the hole. Having the ball sit closer than two feet works even better for me.

THE FIVE IRON HOLE

One of the great things about being in charge of the golf outing is that you get to make up your own rules. (Why should golf be any different than the bar?) Remember, these rules apply to everyone.

It was decided by the powers that be (me), that the fifth hole will be played from drive to putt using only a five iron. Some of the men in the outing could actually come very close to hitting the green with a five iron, providing their directionality (the ability to hit a golf ball in the direction you want it to go) was in the "A" game mode.

At that point in time, I still a relative newcomer to the game, so my five iron shot could actually go farther than my driver, providing I got the ball up in the air, rather than have that pesky grass slow it down. You know, if they would mow the fairways the same way they mowed the greens, I would have a much better chance at getting the ball to go farther.

One enterprising young team comprised of four guys under thirty, decided to use their five irons like a cue stick when it came time to putt. One factor that these fellows had in their favor, and enabled them to lay on the green and get quickly back up again, was, as I mentioned, they were under thirty and still had full use of their knees. The few older than thirty gents that tried this maneuver realized they would put a severe crater on the green when they tried to use their golf club as a cane to assist in getting upright, so they were seen crawling to the edge of the green, (some even begging their partners to pull the golf carts closer), before attempting any verticalization (not in the dictionary) procedures.

THE FREE TOSS

Another fun feature of this "Oh So Serious" golf outing was the "Free Toss" or use of the "Hand Wedge." This could be put into action at any time, on any hole, except number seventeen, (I'll explain later). However, you only had one chance to use your hand wedge, so use it wisely. My foursome watched the team in front of us elect, since all must be in agreement, to use their hand wedge in a situation where the closest shot to the green was only a mere fifteen feet over a sand trap.

It was a humorous display of athletic ineptitude. No one practices tossing a golf ball! The results would have been the same had we just hit the ball with a golf club. One's toss was so weak he would have had better results if he had put it in his mouth and spit it out. His landed in the aforementioned sand trap we were trying so desperately to avoid. Another decided to use a "bowling approach." He failed to give himself enough distance to take the same amount of steps he would take, were he bowling. He kept his eye on the green, started his approach, then suddenly on the third step, he put his foot down, but the ground wasn't there. He walked right in to the sand trap and fell forward. Way to go, Ace.

Now we'll move on to hole number seventeen, and why we can't use the "Free Toss" here? Number seventeen is a par three. One must first hit over a pond. For some of us, this is not merely a pond, but a very strong magnet for our golf balls. Pull out an old, used golf ball 'cause it's gonna go in. If one makes it over the pond, then one must hope that their directionality is in tip-top shape, in order to avoid the four strategically placed sand traps. IF, and this is big IF, your team ends up in one of the strategically placed sand traps AND your team elects to hit out of the sand, then you may subtract two strokes from your team score. Hoooowever, you may NOT use the "Free Toss" on this hole.

If you get caught cheating, you will suffer the

consequences. The penalty for cheating is clearly spelled out on the Rules Sheet, which is passed out to each and every golfer at the start of the tournament. All of these people come into the bar on a regular basis, so punishment could occur at any given time. It states in no uncertain terms: "Get caught cheating and I will spit in your drink."

One of the reasons I chose the golf course I did, other the fact that it was the only one that would take us, is that you are allowed to bring your own cooler and beverages of your choice. Again, this is a bar crowd, and many brought choice beverages. Two guys had to attach a wagon to the back of the golf cart in order to accommodate their coolers. I was amazed at the way some could still hit a golf ball after quaffing down mass quantities of choice beverages, because after the fourth or fifth hole, they were in no condition to drive a golf cart.

Going "Baja-ing" in a golf cart is severely frowned upon by most golf course owners, but this is a really laid back place, and there are no rangers to stop you. I just asked that they not pretend they are driving a dune buggy and stay out of the sand traps, lest I spit in their drink.

By the time we finished the first nine holes, my cart partner, who insisted I drive from the get-go, would tee up the ball, as if he could see the tee, and ask what direction the green was in, I would point, and he would hit. I couldn't complain about the results, they were better than mine, and the strongest thing I had to drink was a Pepsi.

You could occasionally hear cheers from different parts of the course, as teams were sinking birdie putts or hitting incredible drives. Some cheers were simply because it was time for a "Team Shot" of Schnapps. We're such a happy crowd. You would have thought by some of the "ooh's" and "ahh's," and the "oh no's," that this was a big bucks tournament. In reality, one would be lucky to win back their entry fee. The best you're looking at is breaking even. But then, a free day of golf is a good thing. And even more important than the money are the bragging rights. Money only spends once; bragging rights are good for a year--until the next tournament.

ACTIVITIES WE DO NOT ALLOW AT THE BAR

SINGING

Whether one will or will not be allowed to sing at the bar is up to the discretion of the bartender. For the most part, not too many people can carry a tune very well. If I find that you are bothering me, or anyone else, but especially me, I will enforce the "No Singing" rule that I came up with.

Even if you can carry a tune, I may not like your selection of song, so you will need to be quieted. If you are tone deaf, are asked not to sing, and do not heed this request, I may have to take drastic action. You need to remember, just because you are asked not to sing, you should not feel personally affronted. Just because no one else you know has the good sense to tell you that they would rather listen to nails on a chalkboard accompanied by a squealing pig while a dog walks on piano keys than to listen to you try and screech out what will surely be a musical atrocity, even to the hearing impaired, doesn't mean I shouldn't. I just feel it is my duty as a bartender and a fellow human being to stop you from humiliating yourself any further. I knew that after two notes your singing would cause the small children in the dining room to have nightmares for years to come. The neighborhood dogs would start to howl, drivers with their windows open would start to swerve, and glasses would break. Thank God we're not near the zoo!

It's hard to be brutally honest, but some day, you'll thank me.

Three of the waitri were telling me about a song they thought was great. It was called "Lay Some Sugar on Me," I think. It was boldly apparent that we listened to different radio stations. They couldn't believe that I hadn't heard this song. When one of them decided to sing it for me, the other two thought it would be a good idea to join in. They thought wrong. It was not a good idea for any of them to try and sing this song. Three waitri singing heavy metal, a Capella, is NEVER a good idea. When, by chance, this song came on the radio one day, and I just happened to be with one of the Trilogy of Terrible Tunes. She said, "Here's that song we were singing for you!"

It bore absolutely NO resemblance to the song I heard them trying to sing.

As with every rule, there are exceptions.

The first that comes to mind is when, Janice, my cousin's wife, and Vern do their jaunty rendition of the theme song from "Green Acres." If you were paying attention, you'll know that I mentioned this song before. (If not, then you'll just have to flip back through the pages until you find it.) They do it with such an air of jocularity that one just can't help but to get caught up in the merriment! They even have the right amount of sway action, starting with the first word,

"GREEEEENNN" then they crisply enunciated "Acres."

Another reason I encourage this particular duet is to again see that look on my cousin's face as he sits and shakes his head and claims not to know his wife.

STUPID LINES THAT MEN USE (AND SHOULDN'T)

Before I get started, let me give you guys a few tips.

Number 1: If you THINK it may be a stupid line, don't use it.

Number 2: If you think it is the slickest line in the world, don't use it. It will be stupid.

Number 3: If you think you can charm the bartender because you are too smooth to be true, you would be better off just keeping your mouth shut and watching television. Otherwise you'll just end up humiliating yourself. And the bartender WILL share your unfortunate decision to try to be cool WITH EVERYONE!

In fact, don't use any lines at all. None of them work, and they can be somewhat insulting.

For example, (this is you speaking), "If I said you had a beautiful body, would you hold it against me?"

Reply: "Oh, get original! Can't you come up with something that someone else hasn't already used a thousand times? Using an old worn out line just puts you way down on the food chain.

You would have been better off just saying hello. So here's a question to answer your question: Are you desperate or just stupid?"

Another old tired line: "Where have you been all my life?"

Reply: "Avoiding you."

"No, seriously, why haven't we met before now?"

"No, seriously, I've been avoiding you."

And yet another over used, worn out, please let's just put this one to rest line: "What's a nice girl like you doing in a place like this"

Reply: "Kicking ass first and taking names later."

"But I just thought…"

"Obviously, you didn't."

And another….. "Why don't we go someplace quiet when you get off work?"

Reply: ""Why don't you shut up and it'll be quiet now?"

And the list goes on……

"Hey, good lookin', what ya got cookin'?"

Reply: "Witches brew."

"Hey, Sweetheart, we'd look real good together."

Reply: "I don't date men who use more hair spray than I do."

I'm sorry. What's that you said? You wanted to add something to the list? Before you do, please go and reread rules Number 2 and 3, and then think real hard for a few days to make sure you really want to share this with the crowd. This usually saves most fools. After two or three days, they usually forget about it.

SOME YAHOO

Since our building is right in front of a hotel, we get a lot of out-of-town customers. This helps to add a little spice to everyone's lives. Some of these people are here on a regular basis, so they get to know the crowd and are always a welcome addition (like Mach). Every time I see Hector (all six foot eight inches and three hundred pounds of him) from Texas come through the back door, I shout out, "Everyone, lock up your seeesters!" Hector enjoys the acknowledgement.

The ice cream truck drivers are always welcome. They are even more popular when they bring us free samples. One year, they brought us in an ice cream flavor that was only made during the holidays. It was called Winter White Chocolate. Just to keep some from getting confused, we decided that this Winter White Chocolate was an ice cream flavor AND a fashion statement.

Enter one Saturday some Yahoo from Obnoxiousville, Anystate. NO one remembers where he was from; we just knew that we wanted him to go back there. We were all pretty sure that once he left Obnoxiousville, the entire town picked up and moved so he couldn't find them again. Things would have been fine if Mr. Yahoo knew how to carry on a conversation, but instead of conversing, all he could do was brag. Did I mention that Mr. Yahoo's first name was Punk?

Okay, now I have. Punk was under thirty. All those at the bar were not. He made the mistake (and I'm POSITIVE it's not the first time) of letting everyone know that he was smarter than the rest of the free world. He announced to anyone that would listen, and we were down to none, that he made more money than the rest of them, and how he was GOING TO make more money than they ever had because he was smarter and blah blah blah, his ideas were better, he knew how to work harder, he knew which stocks to invest in, something, something, blah blah.

Unfortunately, I was far too busy to stop and take advantage of all this life altering information. Punk also failed to realize that everyone around him had been out there fumbling their way through the work world since he was in diapers. Those on either side of him slowly, and politely, (after all, we're not a bunch of barbarians), started to turn away from him. But alas, poor Betty was having a hard time ignoring him. It mattered not to Punk that she was already engaged in another conversation and had been since he sat down. When he first sat down, he craned his head around to say hi to Betty, and she politely stopped mid sentence, said hello, and went back to her finishing her sentence. When it became blatantly obvious that those to his left were not going to listen to him, he tried in vain once again to get Betty's attention. He kept interrupting her conversation with the Friday Night Supper Club. He then tapped her on the arm. She let out an exasperated sigh and turned in his direction. Before she could get a word out, he boldly announced, "You have poor bar etiquette!"

Betty was speechless, the rest of the Club stared in wide eyed wonder, I stopped and glared in his direction, and he looked at me said, "Well, she does, I'm trying to have a chat with her, and she just keeps turning her back on me."

I stoically told him, "You have a lot to learn about bar etiquette, Junior." His jaws immediately dropped down so low people were counting his teeth. He mouth hung open for so long we were beginning to wonder if the hinge had broken. Helen and Vern had time to make five popcorn shots at his face, each! Well, we're not sure how many kernels of popcorn they actually threw. There was a lot on the bar. I think they were trying to put out his eye.

Then we all laughed. And laughed and laughed. And we even tossed around the idea of setting up a Social Graces Squad to insure that no one else was guilty of practicing poor bar etiquette without a license, but since Vern refused to be the chairman, the idea quickly lost steam.

The moral of this story for all the know-it-all young punks of the world: "If you mess with the regulars, you're gonna get burned."

When are you gonna go out and get a real job?

For YEAAARRRRSSSSS, I had to listen to a multitude of people ask that silly question. Were they upset or jealous because I went to work each evening and had fun? Were there some who felt that my being on feet and running around at warp speed for eight or nine hours a night wasn't like "real work?" Was it not a real job because I didn't belong to a union? (Remember, the Detroit area is a HUGE, pro-union, auto worker town.)

Perhaps it bothered some because I didn't have to drag my half-asleep ass to be somewhere at the crack of dawn. Or was avoiding rush hour traffic (to and from) a feat that one should not be allowed to accomplish?

I'm sure some thought the job was just too frivolous to be taken seriously.

ON THE FLIP SIDE….

You meet a ton of people.

You get great deals on home improvements. Being in a working class neighborhood, not only do we get auto workers, we also had a lot of guys in the trades. I had one friend who worked at the Ford plant across the street, but also did home improvement on the side. He gave me a great deal on re-shingling my roof.

Another owned his own heating and cooling business. When my old, circa 1952 furnace became so loud that you had to turn up the volume on the television when it came on, I decided it was time for a new furnace. Max not only did a great job at an extremely reasonable price, he even gave me a deal on central air and cleaned the ducts for free!

Another industrious soul, who worked the afternoon shift at GM, had a lawn aeration business on the side. He stopped by one day and aerated my lawn. When I asked him what I owed him, he said it was "gratis." You just can't get a better price than that! But add to that the bonus visual when he hoisted up over his head this giant water cooler thermos that had been strapped to the back of his truck and leaned waaaaaaayyyyy back to take a drink, and all I could think was, "OOHHH... C'mon, baby. Pour it all over yourself. Let's..." Well, okay, I was getting carried away, but it was like having a real life Coke commercial standing out in front of my house. I needed a fan.

(Hey! When was the last time that happened to you? HUH?)

AAANNNNDDDD......Another friend did landscaping on the side. (Yes, he also worked at GM.) I mentioned that I needed some rocks to use as a border between my lawn and garden bed, and he showed up one day with a pickup truck bed full of rocks. At the golf course. It was Dan. Did I mention that I needed my old shrubs pulled out? Uh-huh, well, now I don't. How about the new step I needed for the side of my porch, where I made a new walkway once the shrubs were out of the way? Done.

The list could go on and on. I haven't gotten to the plumbing or a brand new kitchen floor yet, but let's get to the real reason we stay on these jobs for years and years. We'll begin by regurgitating the original question: "When are you gonna get a real job?"

Answer: "What?!?!? And give up show business?"

FOR ME, IT'S AN ADVENTURE

Many people, who work in restaurants, are there as "transient" workers. This is just a job to get them through school, or until they can find something else. For me (as the Army says), it wasn't just a job, it was an adventure. A twenty-five year, quarter of a century adventure.

We had a couple of nursing students, (one of the Snot sisters, for example). I used to help her study when it was slow. There were also some future teachers, a caterer, some who went into the world of business, and a few bored housewives who wanted to vicariously live the single life through those of us who were.

I remember one evening when one of the waitri asked me how long I had had my application in. I was slightly confused, seeing as how I had been working here since it opened, so I asked her, "How long have I had my application in where?" She gave me this incredulous look and said, "How long have you had your application in at Ford?"(Remember where we are, the Motor City. I KNOW I'm reiterating. I'm just trying to make this easy on you. You're welcome.) The Ford plant she was speaking of was the one that was practically right across the street. SO, I went out on a limb and asked her, "Why would I have an application in at Ford?"

Again, that look, only multiplied about ten fold, "Doesn't everyone have an application in at Ford????"

"No, I don't. Why would I want to work in a dirty, loud, dingy, smelly factory?"

The look she now gave me, with her eyes bugging out of her head, let me know that I was a LOT more ignorant than I knew I was. She informed me, "Oh duh, for the money and the benefits."

"Well," I countered, "if you make enough money, you can buy the benefits."

I totally lost her here. I do not believe that that concept was ever discussed with her. And then I realized why she wasn't making as much money here as she could. I think she was doomed to hate any job she had and, therefore, left her personality at home. She was never upbeat and happy with the customers. She was under the misconception this was not a "real job." She had to find one of those.

Shortly after that conversation, she did leave to see what

else the world had to offer. I ran into her several months later. She told me she now had a real job. I said "That's great, what are you doing?!?!"

"I'm driving a school bus."

Why wasn't I in line for that one?

WHEN *NOT* TO GO TO BAR

If you have just paid a visit to the dentist and received Novocain, DO NOT GO TO THE BAR. If you do decide to go sit at the bar, any couth you had will forever go by the wayside. People tend not to forget another's interludes of miscalculation of oral adroitness. Okay, fine, you can call it drooling if you want to.

Let me give you an example: Bob, for lack of a better name, had been at the dentist, received two fillings, and God only knows how much Novocain. In all his wisdom, Bob ordered a beer. In all my desire to entertain the rest of the bar, I served him one. Bob had just mentioned to me that he had just left the dentist's office, with that thick tongued, monotonic way of spewing forth words that is typical of the Novocainally (not in the dictionary) impaired.

As Bob, the aforementioned, waited for his beer, he

decided to light up a cigarette. One by one all the other patrons started to glance in Bob's direction. It's not everyday that someone lights up a cigarette by shoving it halfway down their throat. A bet was on. John bet that Bob would burn his lips on the cigarette, although he wouldn't know for a couple of hours until the Novocain wore off, and Andy bet that the cigarette would go out due to all the excess slobber on it before it had a chance to burn him.

Bob smiled moronically as I set the beer down in front of him. Everyone was trying to be discreet, while casting sidelong glances in his direction. Bob picked up the beer. Let the show begin! He slowly raised it to his mouth. Ouch! He banged the mug into his lips! Geez, I hope that didn't bruise or cause a fat lip. He tilted the glass, thought he was drinking, and got approximately half of the beer to go down his throat. The other half was on his chin, and it had quickly made it's descent to his shirt. How charming.

We anxiously awaited the next sip. This time he didn't bang his mouth, but had the glass positioned too high, and he almost poured the beer up his nose. The shirt had gotten wetter. I can't believe he didn't feel that.

Bob had set down the mug and picked up his cigarette from the ash tray. John and Andy sat up a little straighter and payed closer attention. Nope, he hadn't burned himself yet, and the cigarette was still lit. He reached for the mug again. He raised it up to his mouth and WAIT!!!!! He had neglected to remove the cigarette from between his lips! We all stared in wide eyed wonder.No, no one said anything. Why would we do that and spoil a perfectly good moment?The glass met the cigarette, and it was not a pretty sight.

Neither John nor Andy won the bet, since Bob didn't get burned and it was beer that put out the cigarette, not slobber.

Just then, Helen happened to come in the door. As she passed by Bob, she smiled and said hello. She then looked at Bob's shirt, looked at his beer mug with the cigarette in it (Bob has yet to realize that it was in there), leaned over and put her own cigarette out in his beer. Bob's mouth dropped opened, but before he could speak, Helen struck a "Don't fuck with me" stance and pointed at his beer mug. Still clueless, Bob was looking around like a monkey in a room full of bananas, trying to figure out who put the other cigarette in his beer.

A relative new comer to the scene asked how I could serve that guy at the end of the bar, when he was so obviously plastered? I explained that he wasn't really plastered; he just had a Novocain addiction.

When you are in a lousy mood and want to share your mood with others, do not go to the bar. Go to a bar where no one knows you, and then some poor unsuspecting fool will listen to your "Oh woe is me bull shit." They probably won't listen for very long. You're long winded and boring, and we all know your wife. She pays us to let you sit here. No one goes out for an evening to listen to someone tell them what a country song their life is. Be prepared to hear, "Here's a Quarter, Call Someone Who Cares." Don't let the coins hit you in the head.

We're just the happy-go-lucky people at the bar. This place is a world unto itself. The biggest problem arises when there a disagreement as to what should be on the television. Problem solved! We have multiple televisions! See how easy that was? So, sit back watch the football game, and if your team is losing, pick a different team! See how easy that was?What's that you say? You want to watch the Tractor Pull? Go to a different bar. See how easy that was?

When you are already half in the bag, DO NOT GO TO THE BAR.

Picture this: You've been drinking to the point of not being sober (for some, this is just one drink), and you decide to go to the bar. MISTAKE!!! Those who have been participating in the consumption of alcohol are NEVER as clever as they think they are. NEVER! If you show up with too much of a head start, we are going to know it. Drunks are about as subtle as a monkey in a dress doing the catwalk in a fashion show. You are going to stand out. Common sense dictates that we not serve you any alcoholic beverages. Now you are probably going to get even more stupid. You'll make comments like, "Look, I can walk a straight line. I'm fine." Then you'll lose a shoe, which is impressive in itself, since they are still tied. Then, while putting your shoe back on and retying it, you'll get the laces entangled around the leg of the bar stool. It always amuses me when someone tries to push out of the way the leg of the bar stool upon which they are sitting. Then, to remove all doubt from those who are not already convinced that you should get the "Idiot of the Night" award, you bang your head on the bottom of the bar when you try to sit back up.

When you have just finished a tour of the Stroh's Brewery, or any brewery for that matter, DO NOT GO TO THE BAR. We know they are very liberal with their free samples. You should probably just call a cab and go home.

We had a group meet at the bar late one afternoon, so they could car pool to their tour of the Stroh's Brewery. This is for real; they used to give tours. And free beer. Lots of free beer. Needless to say, when the beer is free, quite often there are those in the crowd that may over-indulge. (No, really?) When said crowd came back to the bar after the tour, they were very happy. They were all laughing when they came, and we all laughed at them. One of the wiser ones in the group looked over at me and inquired, "You're not gonna serve us, are you?"

"Uh-uh. You guys already drank more beer than we have."

The only reply any of them could come up with was, "Yup." Hiccup. Burp. "See, I bet all the single women are thinking, 'Gosh, I'd love to take you home to meet my folks.'"

SOME OF THE GREATEST SPORTING EVENTS IN HISTORY

Detroit, and the surrounding metropolitan area, is full of HUGE sports fans, especially when it comes to hockey. There was one particular hockey game that had so many fights, even the goalies skated to center ice to duke it out. These fights were played over and over and over again, and then some. It was so much excitement for one evening. It seemed as if every sports channel felt obliged to show these fights at least three times as much as their competitors. After all, the world of sports is all about competition. AND, each time the guys at the bar saw these recaps, you would have thought it was for the first time. They would point out individual punches to each other, and then they started pointing out their favorite punches.

"Oh, watch this one coming up! See how he gets him under the chin and lifts him off of his skates?!?!"

"Yeah, that was really cool!"

"OH!!!!!! Here's my favorite part!!! Here come the two goalies skating out to center ice!"

"WOW! I wonder if they can even feel those punches

through face masks and seven-inch padding."

"Quick!! Switch to another channel! We missed a part! We didn't see the one guy get clothes-lined! He came right off of his feet and landed flat on his ass!"

All this enthusiasm about sports inspired me to write a little song. This would be best sung by Monty Python and his Flying Circus. (If you don't know who they are, then go educate yourself.) To set the scene, I picture Eric Idle and company, standing in a row, dressed in kilts, and slowly swaying from side to side. (This is even better than golf poem. For real.)

We're mennnnn, we're into sports and this is how we play,

We like to knock you down and bloody up your face,

And wheeeeennnnnn the game is on, can't hear a word you say,

Lest weeeee, should miss the biggest, most important play.

We're mennnnn, we're into sports and this is how we play,

(still picturing those kilts?)

We like to see the mayhem that they all display,

And whennnnnn they're hit so hard that they are in a daze,

We loudly cheer and say that was a super play!

One guy remarked that I had too much time on my hands. I wrote that while I was working. There wasn't much else for me to do at the moment; they were all WAY TOO enthralled in watching the thirty-seventh replay of the hockey fights.

And now for another great sporting event... It was lovely Saturday afternoon. Well, actually, I have no idea what the weather was like, I was inside working. There was a (what turned out to be a BIG) football game on. It was Michigan, as in the University of, versus some Colorado team. The bar was filled, the crowd was happy, their team, Michigan, was in the lead. We are less than half an hour from the University of Michigan campus, so it only makes sense that the crowd is mostly pro-Michigan. Just to irritate the crowd (and to entertain), I bet on Colorado. Think about it. There are no bets when everyone is on the same side. And you thought I didn't understand sports.

Since Michigan was in the lead, this gave the crowd a chance to razz me since I had obviously picked the losing team. But, always having been optimist, I never gave up until the last second ticked off of the clock. There were six seconds left in the game, and it wasn't looking good for Colorado, as the entire crowd pointed out to me. They kept telling me to give it up. But I loudly said, "It ain't over 'til it's over!"

THEN!!!!!! The last play started, Colorado had the ball, when suddenly Cordell Stewart threw a Hail Mary pass and connected with someone in the end zone for a touchdown!!!!!

Colorado wins!!!

"HA!" I said. "Oh ye of little faith! Hey, Boss! (The one with whom I bet), Where's my dollar!?!?!?"

I then proceeded to march that dollar, held high over head, up and down the bar. I'm telling ya. Those Ring Girls at the prize fights ain't got nothing on me! The fact that it was only a dollar mattered to me not at all. It was that I won the bet and the rest of you are losers!

"Na na na naaaaaaa naaaa."

LARYNGITIS

The only time in my life that I have gotten laryngitis, and ONLY laryngitis, was on a Friday night shift. I didn't have a cold, the flu, or any other symptom of anything, but I lost my voice. Completely! I couldn't utter a peep, or an ahh, or an umm. There was absolutely NO SOUND!

Of course, on the plus side, the phone would ring, and there was nothing I could do about it.

Overall I felt great, but it was as if someone had stolen my vocal chords. I found it a wee bit cruel that the Friday night crowd should take such delight in my tribulation. I believe that they were under the misguided influence that they could get in the last word due to my vocal incapacitation. HA!! (middle finger) HA!

So what do you do when life gives you lemons, you make lemonade or veal Picante. I had so darn much fun that night. I never realized what a wide variety of sign language I knew or could make up to fit the moment! And all those assholes made sure that the night was one fuckin' laugh after another. It was kind of them to supply me with challenges the entire night, so as to keep me on my toes, and them constantly on the verge of getting shitty drinks.

When the Friday Night Supper Club decided it was time to order, they went through the usual routine and wrote out their orders on bevnaps. Since they were some of the front runners in the "Let's Pick on the Poor Mute Bartender Contest," I was careful to give their written orders a little extra scrutiny.

Dave and Betty got their order kicked back for poor use of abbreviations. I boldly ex'd out their abbreviation of chick noo, which they use for chicken noodle soup. I told them that this was not a restaurant approved abbreviation. I am the only one who has to read these homemade bevnaps orders, so I let this abbreviation slide for the last six or seven years, but not tonight!

They tried crossing it out and writing over it, but I sent if back again with a note on the back: "Too sloppy. Can't read. Please rewrite."

In an effort to help cut down on waste, I started to save some the notes I had written and had them neatly sitting on the back. All I had to do to make my thoughts known was to turn around and pick up the appropriate bevnap. I had "Dumb Ass" and "Eat Shit" and "You'll pay for this later" and the most fearful of all was a simple "Uh-huh."

Noreen, of course, wrote down "Noreen's Nachos." I had to kick this one back with a note that read "Not a menu item" with an arrow pointing to her self-named culinary selection. When she started to disagree with me, I just picked up a lighter and gave her an expression that clearly read, "Don't make me use this!" Noreen then defensively grabbed her drink and sat back. I rolled my eyes back.

Dave looked at Noreen and said, "For God's sake, Noreen. She can't light Kahlua and cream!"

There are always those in the crowd who are unaware of most of what is going on around them, no matter where they are. Some nights we don't speak, even without the laryngitis. I keep putting drinks in front of them when I feel they are ready, they never have to ask for anything, it's a perfect relationship. They keep talking to whoever is near them, watch the television or observe the rest of the crowd. When they are ready to leave, they ask for their check using the universal sign of "air writing," (You know, holding your hand up and pretending to write on a piece of paper that isn't there, similar to playing the "air guitar"). I give them their check, they put some money down, and I wave to them on their way out.

Then there's the poor foolish soul who thinks losing my voice totally incapacitated me, so they went out on that proverbial limb, and then realize they have snapped it off, with comments like, "Hey, I know you lost your voice, but what happened to your hair tonight?"

Those in the crowd who tuned in on "....happened to your hair," backed off a bit from the brainless dolt that uttered this (what he thought would be humorous) comment, and breathlessly awaited the response. I just looked at the would be comedian with a less-than-half smile, held up the drink I was about to hand to him, pulled out the straw, threw said straw on the floor, and stirred his drink with my finger. I stirred it with my middle finger. No note necessary for this one. Then I set it down in front of him. He issued no further comments.

A lot of people made a lot of comments that evening, and many of the waitri were especially helpful as they walked by with menus and hit them upside the head from behind. At one point, all I had to signal to them was to walk by, keep the menu at head level, keep walking, and get this entire side of the bar, like you were dragging a stick along a picket fence.

Upon arrival, one of the Bobs was feeling particularly rambunctious, which was partly due to the fact that it was Friday. He perked up even more when he found out I would not be speaking that evening. I had to nip his attitude in the bud. The second he opened his mouth to speak (I happened to be turning around to give him his drink), no time was wasted to hear whatever drivel he was going to spew forth. I started hocking, like I was going to spit in his drink. Since Bob considered his beverages to be one of the most precious commodities in his life, he quickly ran his fingers across his lips, like he was zipping them shut, and politely waited for me to hand him his drink.

Give it an hour. Bob would relapse, open his mouth again, and probably end up in "Time Out."

I made it through the night, as did most of the customers. However, the Moron Bros. never even got a chance to sit down. When they found out I couldn't speak, they said they were gonna call their friends. I don't think they have any, but we couldn't take that chance. Dave jumped in and told them we already had last call, and...we were out of chocolate milk. They bought it.

TIPPING

You had to know that sooner or later we would get around to talking about money. Yeah, yeah, I can hear you now. "It's really tacky to talk about tipping." Statements like that are usually made by those of you at the cheaper end of the spectrum. If you cringed at that, you may want to review your tipping practices. Also, I don't ever recall saying "I'm not tacky."

We're not talking about major buckage here (That's money, for those of you not familiar with the vernacular.), usually just the difference between a few dollars.

If you sit down and have a quick drink, it doesn't matter what the drink cost, leave a dollar, at least. If the price of the beverage is $3.50, for example, throw down a five, and be done with it. If you try and leave a fifteen percent tip on a three and a half dollar tab, that would come to fifty-two cents. AS SOON as you are out the door, those sitting around you will start to murmur about what a cheap ass you are, and how they would be embarrassed to come back in if they left a tip like that, they won't want you sitting next to them, you have no class, blah, blah, blah. If you don't get what we're saying here, it would be a good idea for you not come back in the bar. But if you do come back in, and leave another fifty-two cent tip, I AM going to try and put your eye when I hurl the change at you.

All the regulars at the bar get tremendously good service because they understand one basic rule of consumerism, "You get what you pay for." Make no mistake, I also understand that rule. All of the regulars will be met at their chosen seat with a drink as soon as they walk in. This brings us to another rule, "If you decide to change your beverage of choice, that you've been drinking for God knows how many years, then you must do so before you walk by the service bar."

I am not a mind reader. I had one gentleman's drink prepared, brought it to him, and he informed me that he was going to switch for the night. I explained that he failed to inform me in the requisite manner, and he said, "Oh, alright, I'll drink that one, but then I want to switch." He said that like he had any choice. Well, he did have one choice, drink it or wear it.

Okay, back to the money.

Those who drink and dine at the bar will enjoy a multitude of amenities. You will get your drinks faster than a speeding bullet. You will get a full (and honest) critique of the menu and the evening's specials. You will enjoy the camaraderie of those around you. All of you at the bar have primary voting rights as to what is on the televisions. You will get a box of Christmas cookies. You will never be served food that is cold when it is supposed to be hot, and vice versa. If you are not pleased with your order (and if I agree there is indeed a problem and you're not just being a pain), I will bulldoze my way into the kitchen and make sure the problem is rectified. If I think your outfit du jour needs to be critiqued (to save you from further embarrassment of wearing it out in public again), I will not remain silent and laugh to myself. The list goes on and on.

Your basic fifteen percent tip (which I can figure out faster than anyone this side of the Mississippi), would START with basic service. At the bar, you are OBVIOUSLY receiving far more than just basic service, so calculate carefully upward from there. A good rule of thumb to remember: when in doubt, go high.

Sooooo…if you are cheap, the rest of the bar will see what you left, then low rumblings will be heard from said crowd. (I know this is repetitive, but sometimes we don't have a lot to talk about.)

"What an idiot."

"He seemed like a nice guy, but I don't want to sit next to him next time he's here."

"Whattya gonna put in his drink next time?"

"You're not going to be nice to him, are you?"

"That was stupid question. She's not nice to anyone."

"Then why are we here? OUCH! Why did you elbow me so hard?"

Just keep in mind the age-old adage, "Money talks, and bullshit walks, and change can put your eye out."

THOSE DAMN CHRISTMAS COOKIES

Please, spare me the lecture. "You're not supposed to use any expletives when talking about Christmas." You bake a hundred fuckin' dozen cookies, and tell me how YOU feel!!!!

One year, I think it was 1990 something, for reasons known only to a Higher Power; I went on a baking binge. It was a Saturday afternoon, sometime before Christmas. As I looked around the kitchen and saw my assemblage of cookies (I think they were multiplying on their own. I'd like to see the Keebler Elves pull that one off!), I decided to make up a lovely tray of neatly arranged cookies, and bring it to the bar. After all, I had far more than I could eat. Well, actually I COULD eat most of them, but common sense dictates that we not eat dozens of cookies for lunch, or dinner. But if you are having a glass of Merlot, it's okay to eat chocolate cookies, because chocolate goes really well with Merlot.

The cookies were a big hit! I decided right then and there, that next year I would take it a step further and make little packages of a dozen cookies each to give to all the regular customers. How quaint. Then they became "Those damn

Christmas cookies!" Don't get all high and mighty on me again, thinking that one shouldn't use the words Christmas and damn in the same sentence. I bet I can think of a lot of times during the holidays when you did that!

How about, "Dammit, I ran out of wrapping paper!

Or "The damn tape just ran out! Bobby, run and grab me the gray tape, it'll look slivery and festive."

What about this one, that is usually muttered some time in mid-December, "If I hear one more damn Christmas Carol, I'm gonna puke!"

"Dammit, I still have one more gift to buy."

"Stop eating that damn candy, you're going to ruin your damn dinner!"

"Here Mom, have some Merlot!" (Like I said, I got over my severe dislike of wine once I discovered a wine that went well with chocolate.)

HOW FOOLISH!!!! This grew into a real monster! I had to start baking in October!!! The last few years I was doing all this baking; I think I started to look like Betty Crocker. Only it was the old picture of her, from the 1950's cookbook. The one where she had the really stylish hairdo... Oh wait! Don't even go there.

After baking all these cookies, I realized the freezer compartment in my refrigerator couldn't possibly hold all the cookies I was going to bake, so I started too look around for a freezer. I wanted a used and inexpensive freezer. I had to be out of my mind, I was buying a freezer for fuckin' cookies!!!!!! (At least

I didn't say damn.) Its okay, I'm calm now. I just finished the Merlot and the rest of the chocolate chips that were supposed to go in the cookies.

It has always amazed me that, once you get the word out you are looking for something, all you have to do is practice a little patience, and the answer will come. Well, one of my friends, who is actually my cousin since she married into our family, told me her mom knew someone who lives out by her cottage, and that they had an upright freezer they were wanting to sell and that they only wanted a hundred a dollars for it. They told me the approximate dimensions by holding their arms "this far apart" and holding one hand "this high up."

I said, "Perfect. I'll take it."

"Okay, how ya gonna get it home?"

"Oh please, don't sweat the details. I'll find someone with a truck."

Did I mention that where the freezer was is about a forty minute ride from where the freezer was going to? Again, just a minute detail. Remember, seek and ye shall receive. So I was telling everyone at the bar that I found a freezer, and I just needed to get it home. They were thrilled with the news of the freezer. It meant more damn, excuse me, fuckin' cookies. Within a couple of days, I had the "how to get it home" answer. The guy that shingled my roof, Karl, happened to live near the freezer's present location. He said he had to come out my way on Sunday and could stop and pick up the freezer on his way out. PERFECT!

When Karl backed into my drive way with the freezer, you would have thought his truck held the "Arc." I thought the truck had a particular glow to it that day, especially when he opened the rear of the truck and the gleaming white enamel was touched by the golden rays of the sun. (The rest of you should be so happy about a freezer. Then you, like I, will never have a boring day.)

I asked Karl if he had any trouble finding the house where the freezer was. He said, "No, I found it right away. I got out and went up to the door and told them I was here for the freezer, and the first thing they said was, "Would you like a beer?"

Was this meant to be, or what?

We just gazed at it for a moment. Then, he asked me where I wanted the freezer to go. Since there were not enough of us to carry it downstairs into the basement, I told him just put it in the garage for now. He asked "How are you going to get it into the basement?"

"Oh, don't worry, I'll find a way."

A couple of weeks later, for whatever reason, I had a bunch of people at my house. I snagged a few of the young guys and told them if they wanted to eat, they had to move the freezer first. It worked. Thus endeth the freezer saga. Let's get back to the damn cookies.

There I was, neatly packaging up fifty cute little boxes of cookies. (Did I mention that the cute little boxes were Styrofoam to-go boxes that I snagged from the restaurant?) I was baking upwards of a hundred dozen cookies! Do the math, that's a lot of fuckin' cookies!! (At least I didn't say damn.)

Next, I had to put all the cookies that weren't in the cute little boxes, into Ziploc baggies. Did I mention I was a huge fan of Ziploc baggies? I was explaining to one couple how I put the cookies in the baggie and suck out the air. She asked if I used a straw to suck the air out. I explained, "No." She made a very unflattering face when she realized that my lips actually came into contact with the baggie. Oh, for God's sake relax. The cookies are on the INSIDE.

I know what you thinking, "Boy, after all that baking I bet you never wanted to eat another cookie for years!" One would think that would be the case, But no, I still ate the cookies, AND the cookie dough.

Starting at the end of September, Jim, of the Friday Night Supper Club, would have a perpetual bruise in his ribs until the end of cookie season. He would start with his incessant nagging, "Have you started baking the cookies yet?" Linda would then elbow him the side and tell him to shut up. Then he'd continue with more questions and comments. "If you need ideas, I can help you out. In fact it would be okay with me if you just made chocolate chip cookies. I can eat mass quantities of chocolate chip cookies." Linda would then elbow him again and tell him how rude he was being.

The next week Jim would try to slyly slip something about cookies into the conversation. "Hey, about those cookies, if you run out of storage in your freezer, you could--OUCH!" Again, Linda with the elbow, "Shut up, asshole."

By the third week of October, the rest of the Friday Night Supper Club start to place bets on how long after Jim and Linda arrived would he bring up yet another inane comment about the damn, excuse me; I did it again, fuckin' cookies. It was about this time each year that Linda would begin to elbow Jim in the side before they even sat dawn.

On top of the fifty boxes, I also put out giant trays of cookies on the bar for two or three nights in a row, prior to Christmas. Was I a glutton for punishment, or what? (You can agree with on this, but don't call me an asshole, or I'll spit in your drink.) Then there were the larger boxes I packaged up for friends and relatives.

By the way, none of these cookies were actually "Christmas Cookies." I told everyone that I didn't make pretty cookies, just cookies that tasted good. You don't honestly think that on top of all that baking that I had time to decorate them too?!? Get real!! (When I was younger, my brother used to tell everyone that I made Gorilla Cookies. Yeah, he explained that I would roll out the cookie dough, and then instead of using a cookie cutter, I would just stick my face in the dough, hence the name. How rude!)

Here, have a Christmas chocolate chip cookie, or (one of my favorites, off the back of the oatmeal box) a Christmas Oatmeal Scotchie. What's that? You want to know which ones go good with beer? They ALL do, you moron! Do you think you're gonna get a glass of milk to go with those?!? This is a bar. You're not getting a glass of milk!! Not even the Moron Bros. are getting a glass of milk! Be happy you still have a beer in front of you! Now dip your damn cookie in your beer and shut up!!! I'm going to dip your face in that beer if you look at me like that again!

After I stop working at the bar, I don't think I will continue to bake an insane amount of cookies. Not baking probably won't help my mental state, but it'll free up some of my time. Then I can unplug this electricity sucking freezer and use it for old Tupperware storage.

WEATHER UPDATES

One delightful Saturday in the middle of winter, it decided to snow. (What a surprise). And then stop snowing. And then snow some more, and then stop. And then snow so hard it was practically a whiteout! And then stop. This process was repeated all day.

There's an old saying in Michigan, "If you don't like the weather, wait ten minutes. It'll change." That's what it did this one particular Saturday. One minute it could be snowing so hard it was difficult to see across the street, and the next you could be blinded by the glare of the sun glistening on the newly fallen snow. It wasn't much snow, just enough to give the roads a glassy appearance.

Did I mention that it was also very cold and extremely windy at times? Well, it was. It was so cold that when the snow hit the pavement, it would wait patiently for a car to drive over it, momentarily melt under the tires, and then a gust of wind would hit the street, and it would freeze over into nice smooth ice. Its great fun to be at a stop light and have your car move sideways because of the wind and icy roads with your foot is still on the brake pedal. It makes one wonder what direction the vehicle will take off in when one presses on the accelerator. (My fondest wish in these situations is that we not plow into the car next to us, nor they into us. Not to fear. As soon as I get out of the car, my fondest wish will revert back to chocolate or sex.)

Anyways, inside the bar it was turning into a pretty standard Saturday. Anyone who has spent a winter in Michigan learns not to let the weather stop you from doing what you would normally do, but please use common sense when selecting your footwear. Since the weather was such a big topic of discussion, Moo and I decided to give updates every quarter hour, or whenever Moo looked out the window to see if it was snowing again.

Since we thought shouting out our atmospherical information throughout the restaurant was a bit tacky, we make signs. One said, "Snowing," and the other one said (this is a real brain teaser, here) "Not Snowing." The "Snowing" sign even had drawings of snowflakes on it. Hey, nothing but the best. But, once again we had the dilemma of HOW to make sure everyone know that a weather update was about to take place. Lo and behold, Moo spotted some delicate little jingle bells, a long forgotten

Christmas decoration, still hanging by the front door.

It was a simple system we developed. Moo would look out the window, report to me whether it was snowing or not snowing, then she would ring the delicate little jingle bells like a rabid monkey on speed, and I would parade back and forth behind the bar, trying my best to strut like the Ring Girl at a prize fight, with the appropriate sign. After a while some of the customers started giving me weather updates. "Hey, I just looked out the back door when Bob came in, and it's snowing again! Hold up the sign!"

I would reply with a terse, "Don't tell me about it! I can't do a thing until Moo rings the jingle bells. Go find her."

"Can't you just ring the jingle bells yourself?"

"What are you nuts?!?! You belong to the UAW (Auto Workers Union), right?"

"Yeah," he replied, in a somewhat lame manner, I might add.

"Are you an electrician?"

"No," again he replied with the lame shit.

"Well, when a light bulb goes out, can you replace it?"

"No, I have to get an electrician."

"Okay, then what makes you think I can ring the jingle bells when I'm a sign carrier?"

"Point well made. I'll just stick to drinking beer and keeping my mouth shut."

"Good idea, that's what you do best."

But I can strut around while I look for her.

NEW YEAR'S EVE

I always used to tell all the waitri, if you want to be where the action is on New Year's Eve, then work. It's pretty much guaranteed to be busy and hectic, thus making for a night that flies by. Since we don't have any special party thing going, it usually dies down around 11:00 p.m. People come in for dinner, and then go their parties, or whatever. If you waitress, and work until about 10:00ish, then you just killed two birds with one stone. You just made a bunch of money, and you still have time to go to your party. New Year's Eve parties have been known to drag a bit while everyone is waiting for midnight. So much for the waitri, I'm here for the long haul, all the way to closing. (Which is usually earlier than a regular night.)

We always had some of the regulars come wandering in around 11:00p.m. That's when some of the Friday Night Supper Club starts wandering in. Some show up because it's their regularly scheduled stop that day, holiday or not. Others because the champagne is the only free thing they know they are ever going to get out of the boss. It's the old leftover stuff we haven't sold all year. Some of it has had a pretty interesting taste to say the least.

Many a time we've heard one of the customers ask, "What is this stuff? It tastes kind of funny."

"It's imported, shut up and drink it."

A couple of the truck drivers were here for three New Year's Eve's in a row. They told their wives they were spending New Year's Eve with Gretchen again. They told me their wives had responded with, "Oh good, at least she'll throw you out while you can still walk." Mainly that's because it's cold outside, my car windows will be frosty, and I need someone to scrape them off.

Helen, the Ultimate Queen etc., and entourage (her sons and grandson) came in a little early so they could also have dinner. It used to drive Helen nuts because her grandson (he was about seven) liked to spend New Year's Eve with yours truly. Not only did he get more than one toothpick sword with cherries on it, he also got a glass of "champagne" for the midnight toast. All those not imbibing, whether it be for personal or legal reasons (like, you're only seven years old), received a champagne glass with ginger ale. Quite a few times the boss would suspiciously stare down the kitchen help as they were standing there with champagne glass in hand. They would tell him, "Don't worry. It's just ginger ale." Yeah, right.

To help out all the regulars that faithfully showed up on New Yea's Eve, and Mach, because his two month job kept getting extended, I liked to save them the trouble of burning out what brain cells they had left trying to come up with a New Year's resolution and would just tell them what I think their resolution should be.

Betty... Try not to display such poor bar etiquette.

Noreen... Make this the year you try that SECOND menu item

Vern... Try not to...oh never mind, you're not gonna listen anyway

Gary... Here are some animal flash cards I borrowed from my little neighbor. Study and match your Garanimal tags a little better.

Mach...Quit whining about being stuck in Michigan, go put on your ruby slippers and click the heels together three times and say, "There's nothing like a cold beer, there's nothing like a cold beer..." Hey, at least he'll forget about being homesick!

Bob Who Spells it Backwards... Quit smoking, or go back to school and take "Remedial Groveling, 101."

To all the other Bob's... Someone change their name!

To one of the waitri... Use that perfume sparingly, like it was the last bottle on earth.

"What's that, Bob, (it doesn't matter which one)? You want to know what my New Year's Resolution is? First, let me tell you what yours should be: Don't ask stupid questions."

One thing I had always wanted to do, and I get my chance each New Year's Eve, was to line up a long row of champagne glasses, tilt the bottle at one end, and keep on pouring right on down the line, without ever lifting the bottle up again. (Not all aspirations need to be lofty) It's not like I'm pouring Dom Perignon and letting a precious drops spill on the bar. I already told you about the vintage of this champagne.

The getting the champagne heightens the excitement. I tell the boss to hurry up and get all that cheap champagne out here. We only have ten minutes until midnight. He runs to the cooler and starts grabbing bottles. I have the glasses all set up (one for everyone in the restaurant). The old corks would be hard to get out of the bottles; we'd have to play tug of war with them. The one waitress still working has more glasses set up on a tray ready to deliver to those few at the tables. We're still trying to get the corks out. Those at the bar are now telling us to hurry...we get the first cork out...the second cork breaks...there's only two minutes to go...the busboy and cooks are now trying to open bottles...we got another bottle open...Helen is helping to pour...The cook has got a hold of a bottle, the busboy has a death grip on the cork screw, one of them is going to fall...they are tugging with all their might...the busboy hits the floor...there is enough for the first round...We pass out the rest of the glasses...5...4...3...2...1...

HAPPY NEW YEAR!!!!!

Everyone toasts with everyone else! Clink!!! Clink!!! Clink!!! Everyone is happy! I'm amazed we never broke a glass.

"All right, everyone! Happy New Year! Let's drink up! It's time to go! Gimme those glasses back so I can wash them. Yeah, yeah, Happy New Year. See ya next time!"

"Whew."

THE END

CPSIA information can be obtained at www.ICGtesting.com
Printed in the USA
BVOW02s0213250216

438039BV00001B/8/P